Sustainable Development Projects

Sustainable Development Projects

Integrating Design, Development, and Regulation

David R. Godschalk, FAICP
Emil E. Malizia, FAICP

American Planning Association
Planners Press

Making Great Communities Happen

Chicago | Washington, D.C.

205 N. Michigan Ave., Suite 1200, Chicago, IL 60601-5927
1030 15th St., NW, Suite 750 West, Washington, DC 20005-1503

www.planning.org/plannerspress

ISBN: 978-1-61190-120-7 (pbk.)

Library of Congress Control Number 2013943179

Printed in the United States of America

Cover credit: Urban Design Associates, 2012. Courtesy of Grubb Properties and Urban Design Associates.

Contents

List of Tables

Sustainable Development Projects

List of Figures

Preface

We did not inherit the earth from our ancestors; we borrowed it from our children. This adage reflects the essence of sustainable development whether applied to the environment, economy, or the social and cultural sphere. Sustainable land use and transportation is counterposed to the suburban auto-dependent sprawl development that has dominated the North American landscape since 1950. Compact, mixed use, walkable, transit-oriented places offer significant environmental, economic, and social benefits. Yet local political forces, vested interests, and professional inbreeding often conspire to continue the status quo.

Designers, developers, planners, and other advocates for sustainable land use want to embed the principles of sustainable development in their projects, but communication failures among them handicap their work and lower the odds of project approval, given the organized parochial opposition they often face. This book offers numerous ways for these three groups to work more effectively together and produce more-sustainable projects as a result. We focus on simple, straightforward, primarily financial techniques.

Designers use sophisticated approaches to envision land development projects that include "firmness, commodity, and delight," to quote Vitruvius. Developers employ financial models of stunning complexity designed to impress sophisticated investors. Planners create complex development ordinances, often written in dense legal and technical language, to implement their comprehensive and neighborhood plans. Although useful for intra-group communication, these tools and rules are not easily understandable to others. In contrast, the tools offered in this book are easy to use and therefore are more likely to be applied by designers and planners. Better communication should lead to the design, development, and implementation of more-sustainable development projects.

The need for this book sprang from our experiences as teachers of land-use planning, urban design, and real estate development within the city and regional planning graduate program and the business school real estate specialization at the University of North Carolina. We found no text that effectively explained the reciprocal impacts of applying the methods and techniques of planning, design, and development. Yet we knew it to be shortsighted to allow students to focus on only one aspect of urban development projects without understanding the broader implications of their proposals. So we undertook to write a book for both practitioners and students that begins to open the curtains hiding the professional secrets of development finance, as affected by design and planning decisions.

We have deliberately kept the illustrative examples in this book simple, in order to highlight the use of the basic methods and terms. However, the methods are easily expanded for use in more-complex scenarios. Additionally, at the start of the chapters, we have included examples of real-world sustainable development projects, both historical and contemporary, in order to illustrate the range of possibilities for sustainability at the project scale. These examples cover for-profit and nonprofit initiatives, projects with and without government subsidies, redevelopment and de novo plans, and predominantly commercial and predominantly residential mixes of uses.

These sustainable project examples show that the impacts of genuinely sustainable urban development can continue across centuries. The two earliest shopping center projects in the United States—Market Square in Lake Forest, Illinois, and Country Club Plaza in Kansas City, Missouri—were built in 1916 and 1922, and still provide high-quality urban environments. Sustainable projects also can reverse years of urban obsolescence and decline, as old buildings and districts are successfully adapted to contemporary uses, as in Mashpee Commons in Cape Cod, Massachusetts; Santana Row in San Jose, California; Clipper Mill in Baltimore, Maryland; Belmar in Lakewood, Colorado; and Lowertown in Saint Paul, Minnesota. Finally, new projects can create high-quality residential neighborhoods that incorporate both market-rate and affordable housing, as does Bradenton Village in Bradenton, Florida.

We gratefully acknowledge the contributions of a group of colleagues. Jim Earnhardt of Bryan Properties, Inc., and Chad Blackmon of Blackmon Development Associates, PLLC, gave us information on land development cost categories and sources of funds in chapter 5. Eric Thomas, a graduate student in City and Regional Planning at the University of North Carolina at Chapel Hill, prepared the SketchUp drawings of the illustrative apartment and subdivision cases in chapters 4 and 5. Planning graduate students Katie Allen, Heather Schroeder, Paul Winn, Erin Gillespie, Lyle Leitelt, and Sara Reynolds did the subdivision site analysis and plans in chapter 5 during Professor Godschalk's 2009 site planning course at the University of North Carolina at Chapel Hill. Rachel Russell of Grubb Properties and Bruce Ballentine of Ballentine Associates, P.A., provided basic information and drawings for Glen Lennox, our illustrative project for the infill redevelopment case in chapter 7. Ellen Dunham-Jones and June Williamson offered valuable suggestions on the initial proposal. Charles Bohl, Amy Bonitz, David K. Godschalk, and Weiming Lu supplied materials for the sustainable project examples. Timothy Mennel, former APA Books Acquisitions Editor, and Sylvia Lewis, Director of Publications and APAPlanningBooks.com, helped germinate this book; and copy editor Vanessa Mickan and book designer Susan Deegan helped produce it.

We dedicate this book to our wives, Lallie Godschalk and Deborah Malizia, whose unwavering patience and support enabled us to meet the seemingly endless demands of collaborative thinking and writing.

Clockwise from above: *Figure 1-1. Bird's-eye View of Market Square (Courtesy of City of Lake Forest.); Figure 1-2. Market Square Facade (Source: Slo-mo, Wikipedia.); Figure 1-3. GIS Map of Market Square and Rail Line (Courtesy of City of Lake Forest.); Figure 1-4. Site Plan of Market Square, Lake Forest, Illinois (Courtesy of Tom Low, Duany Plater-Zyberk& Company.)*

Market Square, Lake Forest, Illinois

ARCHITECTS: Howard Van Doren Shaw, Edward H. Bennett

WEBSITE: www.historicmarketsquare.com

Market Square, designed by Chicago architect Howard Van Doren Shaw in collaboration with Edward H. Bennett, was completed in 1916 as a commercial center for Lake Forest on the north shore of Lake Michigan. A forerunner of contemporary transit-oriented development schemes, its design places a U-shaped retail mall around a landscaped commons and parking spaces across the street from a Metra commuter railroad station linking it to the metropolitan area of Chicago. Shops are on the ground floors of the buildings, with offices and apartments above. The open end of the U faces the train station, and two towers frame the sides of the square. Conceived by the city as a replacement for an unsightly commercial district, this was one of the first planned shopping centers in the United States. Market Square was listed on the National Register of Historic Places in 1979 as "America's first planned shopping center." It still serves as a landmark center almost 100 years after its creation. The central park space, now owned by the City of Lake Forest and a focal point for community events, was extensively renovated in 2000.

Chapter 1

Introduction: Challenges to Sustainable Urban Growth

Development projects are the building blocks of urban growth. Over time, the construction of scores of individual private and public development projects determines the larger land-use and transportation patterns, neighborhood arrangements, and functioning systems of urban areas.

For cities to work well, their urban growth must be sustainable. Sustainable growth results from development that coordinates existing and future investments in civic infrastructure; accounts for the needs of current and future populations; and balances economic, environmental, and equity demands (Chakrabarti 2013). Achieving long-term sustainability requires that urban development projects contribute to a desired sustainable future. However, the dynamism, complexity, and decentralized nature of urban development complicate the task of those trying to ensure that the continuing flow of individual projects adds up to sustainable outcomes.

Many cities in the United States will have to accommodate population and employment growth in the years ahead. Many urban-area residents have a negative view of growth. The wealthy are able to buy "safe havens" to avoid the negative impacts of growth. This tradition began with the garden suburbs of the 19th century and continues with the gated residential communities of today. But the majority of those opposed to growth try to use the public regulatory process to stop it. Certainly, neighbors opposed to adjacent proposed development have legitimate concerns. They will bear the negative impacts of growth, and these impacts should be alleviated to the extent that it is feasible. But many residents simply oppose growth itself. Their victories displace growth from their communities to less sustainable locations, where public costs are higher and public benefits are lower. These victories may be substantially reduced where developers, designers, and planners work together effectively to propose more sustainable development projects.

There is wide agreement that sustainable urban development will grow in importance in the future, given the demands of increasing urban populations for new space and the impacts of climate change on energy, natural resources, and public safety. Action to achieve sustainable communities is widespread, including the use of sustainability indicators (Feiden 2011) and the inclusion of sustainability goals in comprehensive plans (Godschalk and Anderson 2012; Berke, Godschalk, and Kaiser 2006). The relevant professional organizations have issued policy statements and created programs supporting sustainable development and design: Urban Land Institute, American Planning Association, American Institute of Architects, and ICLEI—Local Governments for Sustainability.[1] The present need is to build on this consensus with practical approaches aimed at seeking sustainability on the ground as new development projects are proposed and built.

Three major professional roles are involved in the creation of development projects, each with its own practice standards and techniques:

- *Local government planners* prepare and implement comprehensive plans that seek to guide future development toward sustain-

1

able outcomes (Godschalk and Anderson 2012; Kelly 2009; Berke, Godschalk, and Kaiser 2006; Anderson 1995). These planners, in coordination with officials and citizens, lay out desired future land-use and infrastructure patterns to be implemented through zoning; subdivision regulations; capital improvement programs; and other public sector actions, policies, and development controls. Ideally, such planning is based on an overall understanding of the economic consequences of plan adoption and implementation at both the community and neighborhood level. At the project scale, the plan is administered through zoning ordinances and other development regulations, requiring that planners become regulators in addition to fulfilling their broader roles (Talen 2012; Elliott, Goebel, and Meadows 2012).

Planners
Developers
Designers

- *Real estate developers* envision and propose development projects that seek to provide sustainable additions to the stock of housing and commercial property in the community (Peiser and Hamilton 2012, Peca 2009, Miles et al. 1991). These developers, in coordination with banks and equity investors, take advantage of opportunities to create urban values through investing in and developing properties. In essence, developers act as urban change agents, finding financial support and taking risks that their projects will be accepted as desirable ways to realize the urban growth contemplated in the comprehensive plan and guided by the existing development standards and regulations.

- *Design and planning consultants* translate development concepts into site plans, engineering schemes, and landscape and architectural visions that seek to carry out development project goals and objectives (Lu 2012, Dinep and Schwab 2010, Russ 2009, LaGro 2008, Simonds and Starke 2006, Lynch and Hack 1984). These consultants, often working in teams, do the pragmatic work necessary to fit the project onto the site, ensure that it will meet professional practice standards, consider its relationship with its context, and enable it to be permitted under the applicable development regulations. Drawing on the community's plan and vision, and the developer's notion of a successful project, these consultants craft alterna-tive proposals for the flesh-and-blood realization of this particular set of structures. They combine specialized professional knowledge with aesthetic values in order to test possible designs against local codes and sustainability standards.

Challenges of Guiding Urban Growth

At best, urban growth management is an uncertain activity. In the market economy of the United States, the engine of urban development and redevelopment is the private sector, and private real estate development is subject to dramatic boom and bust cycles that are outside the control of local growth managers.

Even within local jurisdictions, property markets remain dynamic and complex, responding to unique regional economic and environmental factors. In response to these factors, local development project proposals are formulated and shaped by a loose community of actors, including private real estate developers, their planning and design consultants, and local government planners and regulators. Because these projects are planned and carried out individually, it is challenging for developers, designers, and planners to ensure that they are consistent

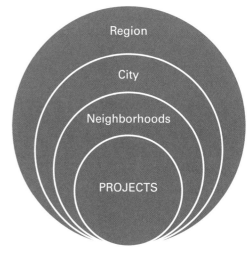

Figure 1-5. Development Project Impacts

with the broader community's sustainability visions and plans. Yet, in the aggregate, development projects have significant impacts on sustainability at the neighborhood, city, and regional scales (see figure 1-5).

Not only is it challenging to ensure that development projects are consistent with larger visions and plans, but it is also challenging to coordinate the actions and ideas of the three major disciplines in project planning. The design, real estate development, and urban planning disciplines need to be closely linked and coordinated to create successful development outcomes. In practice, they often operate in silos with separate methodologies, terminologies, and visions of success: the developer focused on real estate practice, the design consultant focused on architectural and engineering practice, and the planner-regulator focused on urban planning practice (see figure 1-6). The purpose of this book is to connect the silos by describing and demonstrating a basic cross-disciplinary approach to creating sustainable development projects.

An Integrated and Balanced Approach

Our goal is to provide an integrated and balanced approach for creating sustainable development projects. Development projects are complex combinations of building and site design, development entrepreneurship and finance, and development regulations and policies. Projects may fail to contribute to sustainable development when the mix is flawed due to poor integration of these disciplines or domination by a single one of them. Our approach aims to facilitate more-effective integration and balance of the basic creative and analytical processes for formulating development projects.

The central theme of this book is that *the sustainable development project must integrate and balance three major components*:

- *Design elements*—the form, density, and site layouts of new residential, commercial, office, and mixed use projects, formulated by architects, landscape architects, and engineers, as expressed in architectural plans and site plan drawings.
- *Development feasibility*—the financial returns and construction costs analyzed by real estate developers to assess the risks of under-

Figure 1-6. Professional Silos

taking development and redevelopment projects, as expressed in financial models and pro formas comparing project revenues and expenditures.[2]
- *Regulatory standards*—the land-use and public-facility requirements of local government regulations and policies written and enforced by urban planners and public officials to govern and guide the design of development projects, as expressed in development project reviews conducted in accordance with zoning and subdivision ordinances, design guidelines, and public policies.

Our approach seeks to break through the individual design, development, and regulatory silos. To do this, it is first necessary to look inside the silos and understand how they operate.

- *Project design and site plan preparation* is typically guided by professional best practices, design standards, legal codes, and regulations, rather than explicitly by the economic and financial dimensions of projects. The basic goal of this process is to craft designs that will be approved by clients and regulatory agencies; if designs also gain plaudits and awards from the design community, then that represents an even higher level of success.
- *Development feasibility analysis* is typically based on expected rates of return from standard designs rather than from design alternatives geared to unique site and environmental conditions or aimed

at creating outstanding architecture. The basic goal of this process is to propose projects that will be financially successful and will be readily approved by local regulatory agencies; if the proposals also help to establish the developers' reputations and lead to further business opportunities, then that is an even higher level of success.

- *Regulatory review* is typically carried out to implement standards and objectives in comprehensive plans, zoning and subdivision regulations, building codes, and public facility policies rather than as a conscious attempt to use incentives and criteria to achieve design and financial objectives. The basic goal of the review process is to ensure that reviewed projects protect public health and safety; if it also leads to a more sustainable community, then it has achieved an even higher level of success.

When conceived as separate elements, design, development feasibility, and regulation may not contribute to sustainable development at either the project level or the community-wide scale. However, when we conceive of a framework made up of project design, development feasibility, and regulatory standards, linked together by their interactions,

the value of integrating the roles becomes clear. The framework is a triangle in which the three elements are the vertices of the frame, dynamically linked to each other by the sides, which represent the connections between the elements. These role relationships define the *development triangle* (figure 1-7).

Project sustainability depends upon a *balance* of the three elements. If project design takes precedence, the result may be beautiful but may fail in the market and in meeting community sustainability goals. If financial feasibility takes precedence, the pro forma may indicate nice profits, but the result may be unattractive and unsuited to long-term community economic viability. If regulatory standards take precedence, the project may be structurally sound and compatible with the land-use plan but may fail to capture consumers or contribute to design objectives. Sustainability depends upon a balanced development triangle in which all three components support and are integrated with one another.

Balancing the Development Triangle

Balancing the development triangle is not merely a question of achieving relatively equal weights for the three components. It is more a question of balancing the *trade-offs* between the components. These trade-offs can be expressed in terms of competition between the components' goals (see figure 1-8).

The trade-offs between design and development feasibility are exemplified by the notion of balancing project *quality* and *profit*. The competing goals are degree of aesthetic and functional quality versus rate and amount of financial return.

The trade-offs between feasibility and regulation are exemplified by the notion of balancing project *intensity* and the *public interest*. The competing goals are the density, scale, and financial return of the project versus its compatibility with environmental quality, community livability, and safety standards.

The trade-offs between regulation and design are exemplified by the notion of balancing project *flexibility* and *community standards*. The competing goals are community livability, public health,

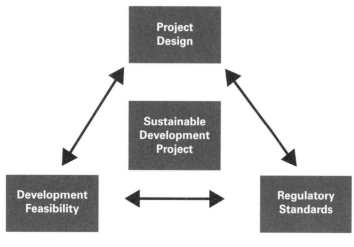

Figure 1-7. The Development Triangle

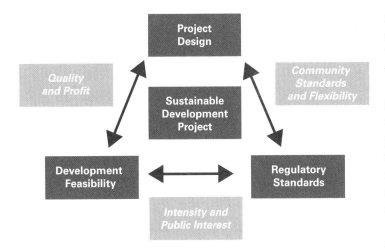

Figure 1-8. Development Triangle Trade-Offs

and safety standards versus degree of design flexibility and freedom to explore aesthetic and functional quality.

We will discuss these goals and trade-offs in more detail in chapter 2. There we will explore the inner workings of each of the three components, including traditional silo-based activities and newer challenges to traditional practice resulting from green design, regulatory alternatives, and expanded public participation.

Plan of This Book

This book presents a process for understanding and integrating project design, development decision making, and regulation drafting based on the dynamic development triangle. It first analyzes the disciplinary roles—design, development, and regulation—in order to explain their insularity. It next outlines a cross-disciplinary approach to balancing and integrating the three roles. Then it illustrates the use of the approach in three types of development proposals: 1) an income-generating rental apartment project, 2) a greenfield residential for-sale subdivision, and 3) a mixed use infill redevelopment project. In each case, design and layout alternatives, including sustainable development proposals that

respect land-use regulations and community preferences, are evaluated against their economic, financial, physical, and regulatory implications. The book concludes with recommendations for creating sustainable development projects.

Summary: Challenges to Sustainable Urban Growth

Cities are built through successive waves of individual development projects that accumulate over time and become part of the evolving urban fabric. While each separate project makes only a very small difference in the future city, taken together these projects are important city shapers. Thus, determining their aggregate scope and character is a crucial act of city design.

The nature of urban development projects is determined by the interactions among three types of actors: local government planners, real estate developers, and design and planning consultants. Local government planners prepare comprehensive plans to be implemented through development standards and other public sector policies. Real estate developers analyze development feasibility in order to propose projects compatible with community plans and regulations. Design and planning consultants prepare project designs to carry out development project goals and objectives. These actors typically operate within the confines of their individual professional roles with their own languages, techniques, and values.

When conceived as separate activities, project design, development feasibility, and regulation may not contribute to sustainable development at either the project level or the community-wide scale. However, when they are understood as a framework linked by their interaction, the value of integrating them becomes clear, illustrating the trade-offs between project quality and profit, project intensity and the public interest, and project flexibility and community standards. The challenges of urban development are to break through the separate professional silos and find ways to balance these trade-offs so that the resulting mix contributes to a sustainable city. Using examples of typical types of development projects, this book proposes an integrative approach for balancing design, development, and regulation.

Country Club Plaza, Kansas City, Missouri

DEVELOPER: J. C. Nichols

ARCHITECT: Edward Buehler Delk

WEBSITE: www.countryclubplaza.com/About-Us/History

Country Club Plaza in Kansas City was developed by the J. C. Nichols Company in 1922 as the first automobile-oriented shopping center in the United States. On 55 acres of land accumulated at a price of more than $1 million, Country Club Plaza was designed by architect Edward Buehler Delk with the car in mind. The design reflects classic European influences, especially those of Seville, Spain, although it does not include a traditional open plaza. This sustainable development project has successfully adapted to new retail trends over the years, initiated the premier Midwest art fair, and recovered from a major flood. Today, it is a major tourist attraction and has become a midtown anchor for Kansas City's Main Street Corridor, linking it to downtown and the Crown Center. It attracts prominent national stores, receives top rents, and produces high sales volumes. Not only an upscale shopping district, the 1.2 million-square-foot Country Club Plaza is also an urban cultural district. Winner of the Urban Land Institute's Heritage Award in 1993, it was included by the Project for Public Spaces in its list "60 of the World's Great Places." Since 1998, Highwoods Properties has owned and managed Country Club Plaza.

From top to bottom: *Figure 2-1. J. C. Nichols Fountain, Country Club Plaza (Source: Wikipedia.); Figure 2-2. Shops along Ward Parkway, Country Club Plaza (Source: Wikipedia.); Figure 2-3. Map of Country Club Plaza, Kansas City, Missouri (Source: www.countryclubplaza.com.)*

Chapter 2

Design, Development, and Regulation Silos

Separate disciplines produce the three components of a development project. Project design is the province of design professionals. Development feasibility is the province of real estate development professionals. Planning and regulation are the provinces of city and regional planning professionals. While professionals in these disciplines communicate and interact with one another, they belong to different licensed and certified professional groups, whose existence is shaped by their members' unique skills, knowledge, experience, and competence.

Each professional group plays a different role in project development:

- *Development professionals.* Real estate developers, appraisers, market analysts, leasing and sales agents, financial analysts and accountants, attorneys, and investors are focused on creating projects that will succeed in the market—that is, whose returns will exceed estimated costs and achieve expected yields. Their plans and decisions are shaped by market analyses, construction costs, and capital availability. Their bottom line is return on investment.[1] As a source of cash flow, a project development is primarily a financial asset in the view of development professionals.
- *Design professionals.* Architects, landscape architects, and engineers are focused on fitting their clients' desired project programs onto chosen sites in an efficient and attractive manner. Their plans and decisions are shaped by codes of professional practice and guided by regulatory rules. Their bottom line is design quality. To them, the development project is a physical concept.
- *Planning professionals.* City planners, plan reviewers, engineers, and building inspectors are focused on preparing plans and drafting and enforcing development regulations to ensure that approved projects are in accordance with the standards and policies of their communities. Their plans and decisions are shaped by legal procedures and the need to balance regulations and property rights. Their bottom line is the public interest. To planning professionals, the development project is a permitted plan for site development activity.

Quarantining developers, designers, and regulators in separate professional silos can result in inefficient and ineffective decision mak-

Figure 2-4. Disciplinary Bottom Lines

Don't silo

ing that produces inferior outcomes and unwelcome surprises when the results do not jibe. Promising designs must be taken back to the drawing board when they do not meet market or investment requirements. Expected investment returns cannot be achieved when site or regulatory restrictions lower desired densities. Desires for walkable and attractive neighborhoods can be thwarted by outdated or poorly drafted regulations, infeasible designs, or lack of market appeal. In essence, the economic and financial dimensions of real estate development cannot be divorced from the physical, and legal and planning dimensions.

The integration of basic development decisions is not only desirable from a community perspective but is also more efficient for the professionals involved. Real estate developers need not waste efforts on infeasible development schemes. Site planners need not spend time drawing up layouts that will not meet basic market or investment criteria. Urban planners need not propose development regulations that will be infeasible to implement. By integrating development decision making across all three components, promising alternatives can be more efficiently explored.

In order to integrate development project decision making across the three disciplines, it is necessary to understand how each functions. What goes on behind the curtain of professional activities? What key concepts and assumptions need to be grasped in order to bring together the work of the major actors? Are there bridging models that can be used to integrate them? We explore each discipline with these questions in mind, starting with real estate development.

The Real Estate Project Decision-Making Process

Throughout the development process, the real estate developer plays the role of quarterback, calling the plays. He or she leads, directs, and coordinates team members, interacts with the public, and contacts potential space users. The development team can be viewed as the producers of space. Consumers lease or purchase that space. The public sector regulates the project and provides services to support it.

The developer needs a general contractor to build the project and financing to pay for it. Financing typically is provided by lenders (as debt capital, also known as borrowed capital) and investors (as equity capital, or invested capital). The developer must also assemble architects, landscape architects, engineers, and other design professionals to generate the site plan, project design, and construction documents. The developer usually obtains site planning and project design services from a firm or consortium of architects, landscape architects, and engineers. However, some large development firms employ designers and engineers on staff.

The developer hires appraisers or market analysts and works with leasing agents and brokers to define the market—that is, the potential space consumers. The developer needs to conduct a financial feasibility analysis, usually with the help of accountants or financial analysts on staff. Legal assistance is required to draft and review the numerous contracts needed to define relationships among team members. The developer may also bring the owner of the site on to the development team, but more usually the site is first optioned and then purchased from the landowner. *option then buy*

Real estate development projects generally follow a basic decision-making process as they evolve from starting ideas to finished products. Along the way, one watershed point is the determination of market and financial feasibility, which is based directly on decisions made during site planning and project design. Only if this make-or-break test is passed can the project proceed through the remaining steps toward construction and subsequent occupancy.

Creation of a typical real estate development project follows a process made up of six to eight stages (Miles et al. 1991, Peca 2009, Peiser and Hamilton 2012). While this process is usually represented as a linear flowchart, in reality it is more fluid and flexible, with continual repositioning and renegotiating, as well as constant interaction, occurring among the stages. For example, the developer has to consider property management as part of the determination of project feasibility. However, the process flowchart in figure 2-5 serves to illustrate the general sequence and scope of real estate development project decision making.

DEVELOPMENT STAGES

1. Inception of idea
2. Refinement of idea
3. Project feasibility
4. Contract negotiation
5. Formal commitment
6. Construction
7. Completion and formal opening
8. Property, asset, and portfolio management

Figure 2-5. Project Development Process (Adapted from Miles et al. 1991, figure 1-1.)

Project site planning and design occur primarily during the first four stages of the process, particularly in the stages of idea refinement and feasibility determination. Project review occurs primarily in the second and third stages.

Stages 1–4: Inception, Refinement, Feasibility Determination, and Contract Negotiation

The process begins with an idea in the mind of a developer, who conceives of a potential project or type of project that he or she believes is worth pursuing. The developer does some quick feasibility tests to determine whether additional effort is warranted. If the use appears feasible at this early stage, the developer finds a specific site and options the land; talks with prospective tenants, lenders, investors, and contractors; and hires professionals to settle on a tentative design.

During the refinement and feasibility stages, the developer hires a market analyst to estimate market absorption and capture rates and conducts financial analysis to compare the project's estimated value when completed to its construction cost. Plans are processed through government agencies for review and approval. The developer

demonstrates the legal, physical, economic, and financial feasibility of the project to all members of the development team. Throughout, the developer maintains an optimistic external outlook, while internally continuing to view the proposal's chances of success skeptically. Peca (2009, 84) advises would-be developers to ask questions about all situations and be critical about market research.

If the project meets development criteria and constraints and receives public approvals (entitlements), then the developer proceeds to the contract negotiation stage. Then the final design is decided, based on what users want and will pay for and what the public requires, and contracts are negotiated. Loan commitments are secured, a general contractor is decided upon, rents or sales requirements are determined, and final permits are obtained from the local government. If contracts are successfully negotiated in stage four, then the developer proceeds to stages five through eight.

Stages 5–8: Formal Commitment; Construction; Completion and Formal Opening; and Property, Asset, and Portfolio Management

Formal commitment involves the signing of various contracts, including joint venture agreements, permanent loan commitment, construction loan agreements, construction contract, land purchase contract, insurance purchase, and prelease agreements. During construction the developer switches to a formal accounting system in order to keep costs within budget, and he or she manages the work in order to keep it on schedule, make necessary changes, resolve disputes, and disburse funds. Leasing may commence at this stage. Upon completion, the project is advertised, leasing continues, occupancy permits are obtained, utilities are connected, and the initial tenants move in. When sufficient additional tenants arrive to achieve stabilized occupancy, the permanent loan is closed and the construction loan is paid off. At that point, the development process ends, and property management begins; subsequently, space is reconfigured, remodeled, and remarketed as necessary to extend its economic life and enhance asset performance.

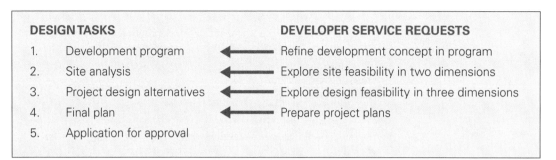

Figure 2-6. Project Design Process

(Adapted from LaGro 2008, figure 1-5.)

During these final stages, site planning and design play a smaller role because the basic physical structure of the project has been determined earlier. However, planning and design may come into play if changes need to be made due to market or other considerations.

Real estate development terminology is unfamiliar to many designers and regulators. In particular, they are unsure of the concepts associated with real estate finance models, such as equity, cash-on-cash returns, capitalization rates, and debt-service coverage requirements. These concepts are discussed in subsequent chapters.

Real estate financial models are routinely used by developers to evaluate project feasibility. However, such models lie outside the knowledge of typical planning and design professionals. If their knowledge base was expanded and basic financial analysis was brought into the project design process and into the crafting of development regulations, decision making would be more efficient, and the resulting products would be more sustainable for the community and better tuned to the market.

The Design Decision Model

Project designers follow a basic decision-making process as they move from initial project concept sketches to finished project plans and drawings. If the developer is the quarterback, then the designer is a skilled go-to player who follows the lead of the developer but whose particular talents make an important contribution to the success of the game plan. Think of an experienced running back or wide receiver.

The design process proceeds in parallel with the real estate development process and connects with it at strategic points. As shown in figure 2-6, the basic tasks of preparing a project design follow a path from preparation of a development program to analysis of site plan alternatives, and then to exploration of building designs and layouts, leading to a final plan and application for local government approval. This is not necessarily a linear process, as the design responds to new ideas and changing conditions over the life span of project creation.

The developer is the designer's client and the source of requests for professional design services. The client relationship typically is based on a contract or agreement between the designer and developer, though designers also work in-house in development firms. The developer initiates the project with a development concept. The designer then refines this concept in a development program that responds to the developer's desires and the relevant regulatory requirements. The program is the basis for analysis of the proposed site or sites of the anticipated development in light of the program objectives. Alternative concept plans based on the program and site analysis follow. The final step is preparation of formal site and project plans for submission to the governmental review agency for approval (Lynch and Hack 1984).

Development Program

The development program outlines the development project's objectives and requirements. The program may also discuss issues of budget, maintenance, architectural style, governmental review, and regulatory standards. Initial program inputs typically are generated by the developer, with subsequent elaboration and testing by the designer. For example, the program might specify that the project is to create a multifamily residential project with a certain number or range of units of a particular type, density, style, and spatial relationship. The designer might outline the allowances for multifamily residential uses under current zoning and note how they affect the developer's expectations and financial needs (LaGro 2008, 14–15). In some cases, the designer might suggest a different development concept, in response to findings of the site analysis.

Site Analysis

The site analysis inventories, overlays, and analyzes physical, biological, and cultural site characteristics in order to identify the site's development opportunities and constraints (LaGro 2008, 13–21; Russ 2009, 47–71). It identifies important site attributes: physical ones such as size, shape, topography, hydrology, easements, habitats, improvements, and history; legal and political attributes such as zoning, building codes, and public controls; infrastructure, including streets, sidewalks, transit, and utilities; aesthetic attributes such as visual appearance, image, and approach zone views; and environmental attributes such as social factors, fiscal impacts, and ethical issues (Peca 2009, 77–79; Dinep and Schwab 2010). It should consider the financial implications of site conditions and the measures necessary to mitigate or adapt to them (Hosack 2010). Sometimes the site analysis will identify constraints, such as bad soils or previously undiscovered brownfield evidence, that are so serious that a major rewrite of the development program is called for.

Concept Plans

Concept plans fit the program to the property. Building locations, access and circulation patterns, and open space and environmental areas are combined to illustrate how the project goals can be accommodated on the particular site. By preparing alternative concept plans, designers can explore big design ideas and explain design possibilities

to clients and other stakeholders. Relationships of building massing, land use, access, and adjacent uses can be diagrammed, visualized, and critiqued. Increasingly, big design ideas involve proposals to retrofit existing suburban shopping malls, office parks, residential subdivisions, and commercial strips in order to create more-sustainable urban areas (Dunham-Jones and Williamson 2011). Exploration of alternative design concepts will be facilitated by the linking of physical plans and development finance analyses.

Final Plans

Final plans are generated from the most desirable concept plan alternatives. After the details have been worked out, the project enters the design development stage, during which specific plans, sections, elevations, and perspectives are prepared by the design staff. Once approved, these plans are translated into construction drawings and specifications to guide project construction and marketing.

Applications for Approval

Applications for approval are submitted to the governmental agency that regulates the project. While the relevant regulations have been checked during preliminary design, this final stage involves more rigorous reviews by elected officials, planning and design boards, and staff planners and engineers. This is the critical make-or-break stage at which designs are assessed against zoning and subdivision standards, building codes, and public policies. Government regulators and decision makers can wield their power to approve, add conditions, or deny project applications.

For typical projects, these design tasks follow an iterative sequence. Designers submit proposed drawings and plans to developers, *← time intensive* who test them for feasibility and send them back for revisions. Programs are revised after developers respond to opportunities and constraints revealed through site analyses. Concept plans are revised in light of developers' financial analyses or regulators' concerns, in order to change the mix of uses or arrangement of structures, or to explore big design ideas. Final plans are developed only after outstanding is-

Differing interpretations

sues of municipal requirements are resolved and developer sign-off is complete. Applications for approval send the project into the local government review process, where it must meet all regulatory standards, committee reviews, and policy tests.

Design terminology is unfamiliar to many developers and regulators, many of whom have only a superficial understanding of the design process and designers' objectives. Terms such as *polycentric development*, *green infrastructure*, *outdoor public rooms*, *human scale*, *regenerative landscapes*, and *figure-ground diagrams* may not convey the same meanings to other people as they do to designers.

This standard project design and approval process, which is the practice norm, involves considerable interaction between designers and private developers and the public. Yet this interaction may still lead to compromised results. We believe that an integrated process would be more efficient and could lead to more-creative, higher-quality designs. For example, Williamson (2013, 63) notes that "the road ahead may require designers to become even more knowledgeable than they already are about real estate financing and pro forma financial statements so as to find the most effective way to argue for the market value and potential return—both economic and ecological—of good design and durable, high quality materials and methods."

An integrated process could also influence the drafting and application of regulations so as to provide incentives for performance standards and development proposals that better meet the goals of local plans and policies.

The Regulatory Process
Urban planning is a multi-stage process, starting with the preparation of plans and finishing with plan implementation. To implement plans, project reviewers and regulation drafters prepare and administer development regulations, including zoning and subdivision ordinances (either individually or as unified regulations combining the two), design guidelines, performance standards, and various development policies and plans. Compared to the roles of the developer as quarter-

back and the designer as running back or wide receiver, the role of the regulator combines the actions of the rules committee chair, who sets the rules of the game, and the referee on the field, who administers those rules. These regulation-drafting and review tasks involve ongoing judgments about how to design and implement the rules of city development (Talen 2012).

Wearing their regulator hats, planners carry out a number of tasks, ranging from creating new development regulations to the day-to-day review and approval of development applications. Needless to say, the way that these tasks are handled has a profound effect on the ways that cities grow and develop. Regulatory tasks include:

- Write, revise, and approve development regulations.
- Review proposed development projects for conformity to standards, including recommending required revisions and potential compliance incentives.
- Administer board and elected official review processes, including monitoring of implementation.
- Feed back information from implementation outcomes into revised standards and regulations.
- Link planning and regulation with development decision making.

Write, Revise, and Approve Development Regulations
The writing of development regulations involves the translation of planning standards into ordinances to be adopted by the local government. Unlike development proposals, regulations change infrequently. Amendments to zoning and subdivision ordinances, including requirements and maps, are made as the need arises. But the basic ordinance content tends to be in place over long periods, perhaps being revised more thoroughly following a major update to the local comprehensive plan. The contemporary exception is when a local government decides to adopt a sustainability-based comprehensive plan or a new type of development regulation, such as a form-based code, or both. When this occurs, the complete ordinance text may be replaced with a new set of rules.

Creating a new set of rules is a major task, often carried out by consultants who specialize in writing development regulations, assisted by local planners, who review and recommend approval of the new regulations.

According to Talen (2012, 7), "the world we have built and continue to build is strongly influenced by specific rules." One reason why development regulations change slowly and incrementally is that they establish systems of expectations about allowable uses of property, and hence expectations about future property values. Property owners, backed by the courts, object to regulatory changes that may lower their property values. A major change in regulations is akin to an upsetting social change; unless it is shown to be a necessary response to a major driving force, it provokes a strong negative response.

Two forces driving regulatory change are: the failure of urban development based on traditional development regulations to satisfy the needs of contemporary society for livable cities; and the growing awareness of the effects of climate change. Advocates for livable cities propose codes that specify the form of desired development, sometimes called _form-based codes_ (one specific version is the SmartCode). Those responding to climate change propose sustainable development plans, with emphasis on both climate change adaptation and climate change mitigation (Condon, Cavens, and Miller 2009).

To create more-livable cities, local governments are adopting form-based codes, which provide incentives in the form of expedited reviews for projects that follow their standards (Elliott, Goebel, and Meadows 2012). The basic premise of these local governments is that codes should regulate the three-dimensional form of buildings and public spaces, rather than the land uses that occupy them. Rules work cumulatively, like "an under-the-radar blueprint to coerce city form, one lot at a time" (Talen 2012, 11).

To meet the challenges of climate change, local governments are adopting comprehensive plans based on sustainability principles (Godschalk and Anderson 2012). Such plans tend to include metrics to assess the progress of the plan in meeting sustainability goals (Feiden 2011). These metrics may be written into the development regulations in order to evaluate whether development proposals comply with the goals of the comprehensive plan. Regulations may include incentives for projects whose designs assist in meeting the sustainability goals.

Review Development Project Proposals

Review of development project proposals involves the analyzing of project applications to ensure that they meet ordinance and policy requirements. It also involves the proposing of revisions to project plans in order to make them more compatible with local development standards. At times, project reviewers suggest incentives for revised proposals that meet planning goals, such as increased density and land-use mixing, transportation efficiency, and reduction in greenhouse gas emissions.

Some localities have adopted sustainability metrics, such as the STAR Community Index, a set of 81 goals and 10 guiding principles published by ICLEI—Local Governments for Sustainability.[2] The STAR Community Index is a rating system that enables communities to evaluate their progress against a series of performance and best-practice measures related to the environment, economy, and society. It applies at the community level.

Others have adopted metrics such as the LEED (Leadership in Energy and Environmental Design) and LEED for Neighborhood Development (LEED-ND) systems of criteria, which apply at the building or neighborhood-project level (U.S. Green Building Council 2012). These building and neighborhood design criteria define levels of achievement in meeting green development goals, ranging from Certified to Gold, Silver, and Platinum.[3] The LEED-ND rating system is the result of a partnership between the U.S. Green Building Council (USGBC), the Natural Resources Defense Council (NRDC), and the Congress for the New Urbanism (CNU). The rating system integrates the principles of smart growth, urbanism, and green infrastructure and building into the first national standard for green neighborhood development. Points are awarded in three categories: Smart Location and Linkage, Neighborhood Pattern and Design, and Green Infrastructure and Buildings. Additional points are given for Innovation and Design Process (for innovation and exemplary performance above LEED standards) and a Regional Priority Credit. No points are awarded for involving local planners in the process.

Other localities have implemented form-based codes, or combinations of codes based on form and land use, which recognize that use remains relevant. Such codes provide more-effective levers to influence both the two-dimensional and the three-dimensional configurations of development project designs. According to the Form-Based Codes Institute, these codes foster predictable built results and a high-quality public realm by using physical form, rather than separation of uses, as their organizing principle.[4] They are regulations, not mere guidelines, adopted into city or county law. Form-based codes offer a powerful alternative to conventional zoning. They address the relationship between building facades and the public realm, the form and mass of buildings in relation to one another, and the scale and types of streets and blocks. The regulations and standards in form-based codes are often keyed to a *regulating plan* that designates the appropriate form and scale—and therefore, character—of development, rather than only distinctions in land-use types (Elliott, Goebel, and Meadows 2012).

One essential aspect of development review is the estimating of impacts of proposed projects. The on-site impacts are handled through compliance with local regulatory standards. The broader community impacts are gauged with various impact studies. The developer hires credible professionals to conduct these analyses. Usually, environmental, traffic, fiscal, and economic impact studies are completed during the review process. The results inform the final decision made by the local jurisdiction.

Development Impact Studies

a. *Environmental Impact Analysis*
Environmental impact studies cover potential impacts on the land, air, and water. Studies of development projects tend to focus on land disturbance, water runoff, and stormwater containment. Because the site analysis directly informs the environmental im-

pact analysis, the design team should communicate with the environmental consultants to share information and insights.

b. *Traffic Impact Analysis*
The type and intensity of use will determine traffic impacts. The transportation consultant will use information from the development program to gauge these impacts. Mitigating traffic impacts with road improvements, traffic signals, and other measures is often necessary to achieve neighborhood compatibility.

c. *Economic Impact Analysis*
Economic impact studies employ multiplier models that assign values based on project cost and size to estimate the output, income, and employment outcomes of the project.[5] Economic impacts come from construction as well as the completed project. This analysis quantifies the economic growth benefits of the project, whereas the environmental and traffic studies focus on social costs.

d. *Fiscal Impact Analysis*
Fiscal impact analysis treats the local jurisdiction as an entity that collects revenues from various taxes and fees and expends funds for capital outlays and current operations. A simple analysis compares inflows to outflows at build-out. More sophisticated work examines cash flows annually until the project is completed and discounts cash flow in order to assess fiscal impacts in present-value terms. The analysis subtracts expected receipts from expenditures to determine whether the proposed project will have a positive or negative impact on the jurisdiction.

Administer Approval Processes by Boards and Elected Officials

The administration of approval processes by board and elected officials involves public presentations of projects, the recording of results of public hearings and decision making, and follow-up actions with

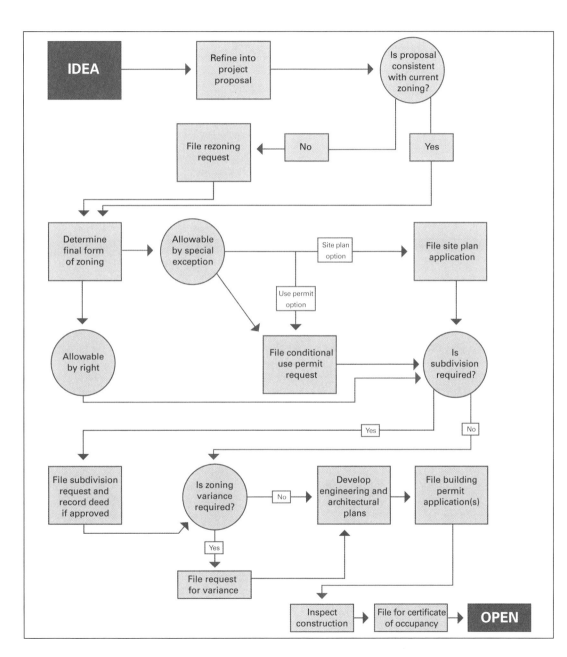

Figure 2-7. Project Approval Process (Adapted from Solnit 1983.)

revise as necessary

project applicants. For projects that have been approved with conditions, the regulator must see that conditions are met before final permits are issued. This task may extend to monitoring project actions and impacts over time to ensure that they conform to the approval requirements, especially with lengthy, large-scale projects. Figure 2-7 summarizes the path of the approval process that real estate developers and design professionals must successfully navigate to move forward with a proposed project.

Rezoning is necessary if the proposed use or density does not conform to the zoning in place. Otherwise, the project could be allowed by right. However, in almost all instances, site plan review is required for the conditional or special use permit. When the site is platted into parcels, the project becomes subject to subdivision regulations that primarily pertain to public health and safety standards, and infrastructure provision. After the project is approved, final architectural and engineering plans are reviewed to be sure they remain true to the zoning and permit received. At times, regulations may impose unintended restrictions on property use. In these instances, a variance can be requested, which triggers an administrative review to provide relief. After the zoning compliance permit is received, the developer can receive the building permit and proceed with construction. If the project passes its final inspection, a certificate of occupancy is awarded and the project can be occupied by its new residents.

Feed Back Knowledge from Implementation into Improved Standards

The feedback of knowledge from implementation into improved standards involves the synthesizing of lessons gained from experience with projects and the application of this knowledge to the revision of development standards and design of new ones. This adaptive planning is particularly important in the era of climate change, when environmental conditions are dynamic and evolving. Because older assumptions about climate stability, energy availability, and plentiful resources may not hold into the future, communities must be alert to

the implications of new scientific knowledge and be prepared to revise regulations as necessary to meet changing circumstances.

Link Planning and Regulation with Development Decision Making

The rules and incentives incorporated in emerging planning and regulatory assessment systems have proven effective in motivating the design and development disciplines to include more green features in projects. However, the opportunity remains to craft rules and incentives that would influence other basic project decisions that could contribute to sustainability, especially those project finance decisions affecting the way that projects are aligned with the city's urban design goals.

Planners are especially uninformed about the process of making development finance decisions. As Bohl (2002, 153) notes in his advice to municipalities on what they can do to support placemaking, "most cities have a 'one-project mentality' and fail to envision the larger picture—how projects fit together to form the city. . . . Use sound market analysis to inform planning and determine what the desired product is, and put incentives in place that will support the desired outcome."

The next chapter will describe a basic approach to linking the three development project disciplines around a common approach to testing development alternatives. The approach includes metrics for analyzing the feasibility of preliminary project proposals and ways to use the results to suggest improvements so that project proposals can do a better job of meeting the objectives of all three disciplines.

Summary: Design, Development, and Regulation Silos

Because of their separate professional approaches, designers, developers, and regulators may find themselves operating in separate realms without linkages to one another's reasoning. Quarantining developers, designers, and regulators in separate professional silos can result in inefficient and ineffective decision making that produces inferior outcomes and unwelcome surprises when the results do not jibe with expectations.

Each realm has its own measures of success. Development professionals are focused on creating projects that will succeed in the market. Their bottom line is return on investment. Design professionals are focused on fitting their clients' desired project programs onto chosen sites in an efficient and attractive manner. Their bottom line is design quality. Planning professionals are focused on preparing plans and drafting and enforcing development regulations that will ensure that approved projects are in accordance with the standards and policies of their communities. Their bottom line is the public interest.

Developing methods of analysis and ways of thinking that cross over professional silos can help to ensure development projects that better meet the needs of each set of actors and produce outcomes that are greener, more efficient, and more sustainable. By putting themselves in the shoes of the others, developers can achieve higher design quality, designers can achieve better returns on investment, and planners can further the public interest through setting standards and rules that recognize and provide incentives for better and more rewarding projects.

From top to bottom: *Figure 3-1. Clock Tower on Signature Building, Mashpee Commons (Courtesy of Charles C. Bohl.); Figure 3-2. Liner Buildings Fronting Parking Lot, Mashpee Commons (Courtesy of Charles C. Bohl.); Figure 3-3. Master Plan of Mashpee Commons, Cape Cod, Massachusetts (Courtesy of Cornish Associates LLP.)*

Mashpee Commons, Cape Cod, Massachusetts

DEVELOPER: Cornish Associates Limited Partnership

MASTER PLANNERS AND PRIMARY BUILDING ARCHITECTS: Imai Keller Moore Architects

CHARRETTE PLANNER: Duany Plater-Zyberk & Company

WEBSITE: http://cornishlp.com/mashpee-commons

Mashpee Commons, a mixed use downtown center on 140 acres, is the earliest retrofit of a suburban strip center in the United States. Started in 1986, this groundbreaking redevelopment project replaced a 75,000-square-foot center with 460,000 square feet of new commercial uses and 482 residential units. The developer's challenge was to introduce a high-density, mixed use project into Cape Cod's "no growth" environment and cumbersome local zoning, which forced a multiyear evolutionary approval and development process. During some two decades, large sections of the existing center were demolished and rebuilt in stages, adjacent residential neighborhoods have been planned to connect to the walkable village center, new wastewater treatment facilities were built, and a new transit node was created. Design charrettes in 1988 and 2002 established the center's master plan and the layout of abutting residential neighborhoods with small lots and attached housing. Mashpee Commons is based on traditional neighborhood design. Its innovative features include residential-above-retail buildings, incorporation of civic uses, and 20-foot-deep liner buildings that front parking areas with shallow retail shops.

Chapter 3

Linking Project Design, Development, and Regulation

Underlying all development-triangle decisions is the root issue of *feasibility.* Feasible development projects appear to be reasonable, seem suitable for the intended uses, and ultimately can be carried out. All proposed real estate development projects must be able to satisfactorily answer the three basic feasibility questions that pertain to the triangle:

[handwritten: 3. step feasibility Test]

- Is the project design feasible?
- Is the project development finance scheme feasible?
- Is the project feasible in regard to regulatory compliance?

These are not simple questions. Answering them requires meeting not only intra-disciplinary standards but also interdisciplinary standards. A project design must meet regulatory and return-on-investment requirements as well as architectural and engineering requirements. A real estate development scheme must meet design and regulatory requirements as well as equity-return requirements. And regulatory ordinances and reviews cannot ignore project design and finance requirements when community-wide development policies and plans are implemented.

The design and regulation perspectives put emphasis on the physical feasibility of the project. The regulators apply public interest criteria as expressed in legally binding zoning that defines the development envelope of a site. Designers work within this legally defined development envelope to achieve the design quality they seek and the developer's program of land and space use. These feasible outcomes rarely maximize the physical capacity of the site but do reflect the intensity that is politically possible in the jurisdiction.

Beyond physical and legal feasibility, the factor that determines whether a project is *successfully developed* is its ultimate economic and financial feasibility. There are many unfortunate examples of projects that met the design and regulatory feasibility tests but failed to meet the market test. Success in the market is determined by many factors besides developer judgment about the development scheme, including local supply-and-demand conditions, emerging trends in space use, business and building cycles, and project timing. However, those who comprehensively preview the impacts of a project and then revise components interactively to improve feasibility before final decisions are made increase their chances of satisfying design, development, and regulatory feasibility requirements.

For such a preview and revision process, we propose two straightforward economic and financial techniques that can account for interactions between project design, development, and regulation: *cost-driven analysis* and *market-driven analysis.* The advantages of these related techniques are their ease of use, relative to more complex financial models; their capacity to assess the impacts of project revisions with limited data gathering; and their clear logic, which appeals to those with limited financial analysis skills. They are useful in demystifying the sometimes arcane field of development project finance. This chapter describes these techniques and illustrates their combined application potential with an example based on an apartment project.

Cost-Driven and Market-Driven Financial Analyses

During project inception, developers employ back-of-the-envelope techniques to gauge whether additional time, effort, and funds should be devoted to the project under consideration. Usually, they are evaluating several project options simultaneously. If an idea seems promising, it is refined further and compared to other project options under review. As a way to transition to a more formal feasibility analysis, the developer works with the designer to articulate the development program to address the physical and legal dimensions of feasibility. The developer then begins to "run the numbers" to address the economic and financial dimensions. The fundamental question the developer asks at this stage is Under what conditions would the proposed project become viable? To address the economic and financial dimensions, both current and future conditions bear upon estimated project cost and estimated project value.

Cost-driven and market-driven analyses can be used to answer the refinement question in a time-effective and cost-effective manner. They are static techniques that are less comprehensive and complicated than discounted cash flow analysis, which is a dynamic and information-intensive technique (see chapter 6). The attractiveness of static cost-driven and market-driven analyses stems from their reliance upon limited amounts of readily available information. Because of the level of effort they require, they are ideal ways to determine whether it is worth pursuing formal feasibility work.

Cost-driven analysis asks whether the estimated costs of the project will allow adequate returns from rent or sales. Market-driven analysis asks the question the other way: Will the estimated returns from rent or sales justify the cost of the project? The analyst uses each technique to check on the accuracy and logic of the other technique and to identify ways to improve overall feasibility. Figure 3-4 presents the logic and elements of these techniques.

Cost-Driven Approach
Do the costs permit adequate returns?

SPACE PRODUCER

Acquisition and Construction
Development Envelope Analysis
Capital Budget (Land, Hard, and Soft Costs)
Financial Plan (Equity and Debt Capital Requirements)

Financing
Measures of Risk and Return:
Loan-to-Cost Ratio
Debt-Service Coverage Ratio
Mortgage Constant
Before Tax Cash-on-Cash Returns

Operations
Operating Budget (Operating Expenses and Real Estate Taxes)
Vacancy Rate
Revenue Levels

Market
Market Analysis (Users, Sales Prices, and Rent Levels)

SPACE CONSUMER

Do the returns justify the costs?
Market-Driven Approach

Figure 3-4. Cost-Driven and Market-Driven Approaches to Development Feasibility (Ciochetti and Malizia 2000, 140; and the authors.)

Cost-driven analysis begins with a calculation of the costs of site acquisition, construction, financing, and operations so that the necessary rent level for the project can be derived. *Market-driven analysis* begins with a calculation of market rents and operating expenses to arrive at the justifiable capital budget and residual funds available to purchase the land (Graaskamp 1970, 1981; Ciochetti and Malizia 2000). The relevant terms are defined in the glossary of real estate terms. The appendix to this chapter explains the specific factors and the arithmetic for each approach.

The logic behind cost-driven analysis is worth explaining. The capital budget amount must be financed to purchase the site and to construct the project. The lender will underwrite the project at some loan-to-cost ratio (50–80 percent) depending on the viability of the project, experience of the development team, and general economic conditions. The rest of the financing must come from investors.

To obtain debt and equity financing, the project must ultimately generate adequate returns. Debt service is both the return *on* capital (interest portion) and return *of* capital (principal portion) that satisfies the lender. The required cash return to investors is the annual payment needed to meet their return expectations (cash-on-cash return). Together, these payments equal the *minimum* amount of net operating income (NOI) needed to satisfy the lender and investors.

How much revenue is needed to generate this amount of NOI? Adding estimates of operating expenses and real estate taxes yields effective gross income. Adding estimated vacancy loss gives gross potential revenue. Dividing this amount by the units or square footage available to rent gives the minimum rent level needed to generate this amount of NOI. Market rent below this level will not provide enough revenue to purchase the site and build the project.

Market-driven analysis moves in the opposite direction to estimate the capital budget that market rents can support (see appendix to this chapter).

The logic of market-driven analysis parallels that of cost-driven analysis. Given market rent levels, estimated NOI is the *maximum* amount of annual cash flow expected from the project. This amount is distributed first to the lender in the form of debt service. Then the remainder goes to investors. Applying the cost of debt (mortgage

constant) and cost of equity (cash-on-cash return rate) to these distributions gives the maximum amount of debt and equity capital available for the project (the justified project investment).

How much can be paid for the site with this justified project investment? Hard costs, soft costs, and site development costs are the costs of improvements that must be deducted from the justified project investment. The positive residual is the maximum amount that can be paid for the site, given market rent levels. It represents what the site is worth—its fair market value—under this development scenario. The asking price for the site may be higher or lower than the residual. A negative residual indicates an infeasible project, because the capital improvements cannot be covered, and no cash is available for the site.

Although real estate markets are not very efficient, it is rare that cost-driven analysis will generate rents below current market rents or that market-driven analysis will provide sufficient cash to cover the asking price of the land. Usually, the project appears to be financially infeasible. The question is, by how much? Projects that are almost feasible deserve further analysis. Developers make this judgment on the basis of past experience, current market conditions, and future prospects. Projects with required rent 15–30 percent above actual rent or justified capital budgets covering 70–80 percent of all-in project costs usually deserve further attention. Those within 10 percent of rents or 90 percent of costs are generally quite attractive. Since developers are simultaneously evaluating more than one project option, they make relative comparisons and select the best alternative.

The cost estimates used in cost-driven and market-driven analyses should not change much before project construction begins (presumably within the same year). However, the rents and expenses may well change between the present and the time when the project receives its certificate of occupancy. If the market is expected to remain the same or weaken, feasibility would not improve. But if the market is expected to be stronger when the project is completed—say, in two to three years—the project would become more feasible. The point is that because cost-driven and market-driven analyses are static techniques, they ignore potential financial benefits from income growth and property appreciation that may occur over time. These benefits are captured in *discounted cash flow analysis*, which is discussed in chapter 6. From this perspective, cost-driven and market-driven analyses offer conservative tests of financial feasibility.

For preliminary analysis of a development project proposal, the static approach of market-driven and cost-driven techniques can show whether the project concept is in the ballpark. This may be sufficient to indicate whether project refinements should be pursued or the development strategy should be totally revised. The following illustrative application to the development program of an apartment project demonstrates how the techniques can be used.

Illustrative Application: Analysis of Apartment Project Development Program

The development program is the game plan for development—a written document that outlines the objectives and requirements for a winning project, as well as the potential obstacles to success. The development program explains the nature of the proposed project, including its type and size, its site, the applicable development regulations, its design, and salient budget issues. Site analyses, concept plans, and final designs, which are covered in later chapters, flow from the development program.

Elements of a Project Development Program

The development program describes the nature of the project that is envisioned. It should provide enough detail to enable the preparation and evaluation of concept plans and designs. Elements might include:

a. *Project Type*
   Proposed uses: residential (multifamily, single-family), commercial (office, retail, shopping center), industrial (manufacturing, processing, warehouse, flex space), public (park, recreation, public facility, government office), mixed use (office-commercial, residential-commercial-office)

b. *Project Size*
   Size of overall project (number of housing units, square feet of office or other commercial), building height (number of stories), number of establishments (stores, offices), amount of parking (square feet of surface lots or decks, number of spaces)

c. *Site*
   Property size (acres, square feet), location (address, coordinates), tax identification number, neighborhood, utility availability (water, wastewater), road access, topography, use history, streams, floodplains, other hazards or development constraints

d. *Regulations*
   Zoning district requirements (relating to density, setbacks, floor area ratio, and so on), subdivision ordinance requirements (relating to open space, lot size, infrastructure provision, and so on), governmental reviews, public hearings

e. *Design*
   Desired architectural style (such as traditional or contemporary), site design (such as grid street pattern or organic layout)

f. *Budget Issues*
   Constraints on total expenditures or specific expenditures for amenities, site work, open space, construction quality, and so on.

As indicated in the real estate development model described in chapter 2, the development program takes shape in the mind of the developer during idea inception (stage 1) and is fleshed out during the refinement stage (stage 2), when expectations and preferences for the type, size, and style of the project begin to be articulated. The development program bridges idea refinement and project feasibility (stage 3). Design professionals expand and refine the developer's initial program to address the physical and legal dimensions of the project. These refinements feed into the financial analysis.

During the project refinement and feasibility stages, the developer assembles the development team and takes the project through the development review process. At the conclusion of this stage, two feasibility decisions are made; one is financial, and the other is political. The developer decides whether the project is sufficiently profitable to justify its development; and the local jurisdiction decides whether the project achieves public objectives and meets regulatory requirements. If so, the developer receives the requested entitlements. If the project is a "go," the developer continues the feasibility analysis (stage 3) and contract negotiations (stage 4), and completes formal commitments (stage 5) that lead to the initiation of construction (stage 6).

The initial development program typically is fluid and goes through revision as more is learned about the project in its political, social, and environmental settings. The program is elaborated and tested by the design team in light of existing physical conditions and regulatory standards. The developer and designer may engage in extensive dialogue before a final program is agreed upon. Later on, they may consider findings from the succeeding site-analysis stage or development regulations that can cause the development program to change. During the program-formation process, opportunities exist for review of the financial impacts of program alternatives and the revision of the development strategy to achieve better development outcomes.

A number of books offer in-depth guidance on program preparation (Russ 2009, LaGro 2008, Lynch and Hack 1984). This chapter is not about the mechanics of preparing a development program, but rather how a program can be explored using static analytical techniques. To demonstrate this, we analyze the development implications of a hypothetical program for an apartment project.

Developers who move successfully from idea inception to stabilized occupancy have learned how to manage development risk. One important risk-management tool is the conversion of assumption and speculation to data and facts (Graaskamp 1981). Thus, idea refinement and feasibility analysis themselves are risk-management tools. The development program formulates a contingency plan that changes with the application of what-if questions. The answers to these questions have important implications for potential financial returns and development risk.

In this illustrative base case, assume that a developer believes that an apartment project may provide a development opportunity.

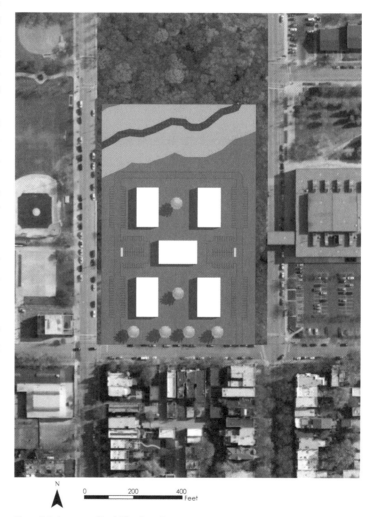

Figure 3-5. Apartment Sketch Plan: Base Case

An option has been procured on a 12.5-acre property zoned for multifamily uses, located in an urban area, and served by existing streets and utilities. The property has an existing stream and floodplain at the rear. The assumed initial program objective is to build a multifamily residential project with 100 two-bedroom rental units, at a net density of eight units to the acre, arranged around a central open space with surface parking lots on the periphery. The first design sketch proposes five two-story buildings, each with 20 apartment units. Parking is provided at a ratio of 1.5 spaces per apartment unit (see figure 3-5).

Table 3-1 provides the cost and revenue estimates and other parameters that are needed to conduct cost-driven and market-driven analyses for this illustrative case. For the baseline case, the five buildings result in 130,500 square feet of construction. Given an efficiency ratio of about 92 percent, the net leasable area is 120,000 square feet, or 1,200 square feet per apartment unit on average. The 12.5-acre site costs about $1.36 million to purchase. Site development costs are $64,000 per acre. Hard costs are estimated at $142,800 per unit ($119 per square foot). Soft costs are 20 percent of hard costs, or $23.80 per square foot. Hard costs, soft costs, and site development costs amount to $19.44 million. The total development cost when the cost of the site is included is almost $21 million.

The lender is willing to offer financing at a loan-to-cost ratio of 0.75 and debt-service coverage ratio of 1.15. Financing terms are: 6 percent interest, monthly payments, 20-year term, and a call provision after seven years that indicates when the borrower may have to pay the remaining loan balance. Given these loan terms, the calculated annualized monthly mortgage constant is 0.085972. Equity sources are willing to invest for a 12 percent cash-on-cash return.

Operating expenses and real estate taxes combined are about $5,600 per unit per year ($2.75 per square foot plus real estate taxes of $12 per $1,000 of assessed value, which is assumed to equal the total development cost). The market rent per unit is assumed to be $1,800 per month, or $21,600 per year ($1.50 per square foot per month, or $18 per square foot per year). Vacancies for the project are set at 5 percent.

TABLE 3-1. REVENUES, COSTS, AND PARAMETERS: BASE CASE

INPUTS	BASE CASE
Building in SF	130,500
Efficiency Ratio	0.91954
Net Leasable Area in SF	120,000
Site in SF (Ac)	544,500 (12.5)
Land Cost per SF	$2.50
Land Cost	$1,361,250
Site Development Costs, Total (per Ac)	$800,000 ($64,000)
Hard Costs per SF	$119
Soft Costs per SF at 20% of Hard Costs	$23.80
Hard Costs	$15,529,500
Soft Costs	$3,105,900
Capital Budget without Land	$19,435,400
Total Development Cost	$20,796,650
Annualized Monthly Mortgage Constant	0.085972
Loan-to-Cost Ratio	0.75
Debt-Service Coverage Ratio	1.15
Cash-on-Cash Return	0.12
Operating Expenses per SF	$2.75
Real Estate Taxes per $1,000	$12
Rent per SF per Year (Month)	$18 ($1.50)
Other Income per SF per Year	$0.25
Total Revenue per SF per Year	$18.25
Vacancy Rate	0.05
Unit Size in SF	1,200
Total Units	100

TABLE 3-2. COST-DRIVEN ANALYSIS USING LOAN-TO-COST RATIO: BASE CASE

COSTS

COSTS	
Acquisition	$1,361,250
Hard Costs	$15,529,500
Soft Costs	$3,105,900
Site Development	$800,000
Total Development Cost	$20,796,650

EQUITY

EQUITY	
1 Minus Loan-to-Cost Ratio	0.25
x Total Development Cost	$20,796,650
= Equity Needed	$5,199,163
x Cash-on-Cash Return Rate	12%
= Required Cash Returns	$623,900

DEBT

DEBT	
Total Development Cost	$20,796,650
x Loan-to-Cost Ratio	0.75
= Allowable Mortgage Amount	$15,597,488
x Annualized Monthly Mortgage Constant	0.0859720
= Annual Debt Service	$1,340,947

Cash Returns + Debt Service = NOI

Debt-Service Coverage Ratio = 1.47

Net Operating Income (NOI)	$1,964,847
+ Operating Expenses	$358,875
+ Real Estate Taxes	$249,560
= Effective Gross Income	$2,573,281
+ Vacancy	$135,436
= Gross Required Revenue	$2,708,717
÷ Net Leasable Area in SF	120,000
= Required Rental Income per SF	$22.57
Market Rent	$18.25
Required Rent / Market Rent	124%

TABLE 3-3. MARKET-DRIVEN ANALYSIS USING DEBT-SERVICE COVERAGE RATIO: BASE CASE

Market Rent	$18.25
× Net Leasable Area in SF	120,000
= Gross Potential Revenue	$2,190,000
− Vacancy	$109,500
= Effective Gross Income	$2,080,500
− Operating Expenses	$358,875
− Real Estate Taxes	$249,560
Net Operating Income (NOI)	$1,472,066

EQUITY

Net Operating Income (NOI)	$1,472,066
− Debt Service	$1,280,057
= Cash Available for Investors	$192,009
÷ Cash-on-Cash Return Rate	12%
= Justified Equity Investment	$1,600,071

DEBT

Net Operating Income (NOI)	$1,472,066
÷ Debt-Service Coverage Ratio	1.15
= Cash Available for Debt Service	$1,280,057
÷ Annualized Monthly Mortgage Constant	0.0859720
= Justified Mortgage Amount	$14,889,232

Loan to Cost Ratio = 0.72

Equity Investment + Mortgage Amount = JPI

Justified Project Investment (JPI)	$16,489,303
− Total Development Cost without Land	$19,435,400
= Justified Land Purchase Price	$2,946,097
Land Cost	$1,361,250
Additional Funds Required	$4,307,347
Justified Investment / Total Development Cost	79.29%

The cost-driven analysis indicates that the required rent is 24 percent over market (see table 3-2). The market-driven analysis finds that the justified project investment of about $16.5 million is less than the anticipated capital budget without land, $19.4 million (see table 3-3). Therefore, additional funding of more than $4.3 million is needed to build the project and purchase the land. This base case does not represent a feasible project.

Given the results of the thorough cost-derived and market-derived analyses, the base case does not look promising, and substantial project revisions are called for. To explore other possibilities, the design team might review the zoning regulations and other design guidelines or rules that are in effect. The developer might use market and financial information gathered during this stage to consider the financial implications of program modifications under these contingencies. The planners might seize the opportunity afforded by an infeasible base case to offer regulations, performance standards, or incentives that achieve smart growth or sustainable development objectives by increasing the project's design quality and financial feasibility. These alternatives are explored and analyzed in chapter 4.

Summary: Linking Project Design, Development, and Regulation

Underlying all development decisions is the root issue of feasibility. Proposed real estate development projects must be able to answer yes to questions of whether the project design, development finance, and regulatory compliance are all feasible. Those who comprehensively preview the impacts of a project and then revise components interactively to improve feasibility before final decisions are made increase their chances of satisfying design, development, and regulatory feasibility requirements.

Two straightforward economic and financial techniques can account for interactions between project design, development, and regulation: cost-driven analysis and market-driven analysis. These techniques are relatively easy to apply, can be used to assess the impacts of project revisions with limited data gathering, and follow a clear logic. They are useful in demystifying the sometimes arcane field of development project finance. Cost-driven analysis asks whether the estimated costs of the project will allow adequate returns from rent or sales. Market-driven analysis asks the question the other way: will the estimated returns from rent or sales justify the cost of the project? The analyst uses each technique to check on the accuracy and logic of the other technique and to identify ways to improve overall feasibility.

The analyses are applied to an illustrative base case: an apartment project on a 12.5-acre property zoned for multifamily uses, located in an urban area, and served by existing streets and utilities. The property has an existing stream and floodplain at the rear. The initial program objective is to build 100 two-bedroom rental units at a gross density of eight units to the acre, arranged around a central open space with surface parking lots on the periphery. The first design sketch proposes five two-story buildings, each with 20 apartment units, and parking at 1.5 spaces per unit.

In this illustrative case, the cost-driven analysis indicates that the required rent is 24 percent over market. The market-driven analysis finds that the justified project investment of about $16.5 million is less than the anticipated capital budget without land of $19.4 million. Therefore, additional funding of more than $4.3 million is needed to build the project and purchase the land. Based on these analyses, this base case does not represent a feasible project, and the design needs to go back to the drawing board.

Appendix to Chapter 3

Cost-Driven Analysis Arithmetic

For cost-driven analysis, the cost of the site plus site development costs, hard costs, and soft costs yield the total development cost.

Site Acquisition Cost + Site Development Costs + Hard Costs + Soft Costs = Total Development Cost

Financing terms dictate how much debt can be raised (the loan-to-cost ratio) to finance the project. Multiplying this ratio by the total development cost gives the mortgage loan amount.

Total Development Cost × Loan-to-Cost Ratio = Allowable Mortgage Amount

The mortgage constant is the annual cost of debt per dollar of the original loan balance. Multiplying the mortgage constant by the original amount of the loan yields the annual debt service.

Allowable Mortgage Amount × Annualized Mortgage Constant = Annual Debt Service

The remaining amount of financing is the difference between the total development cost and the mortgage loan. This amount must be raised in the form of equity capital.

Total Development Cost – Mortgage Amount = Cash Equity Requirement

Developers usually know the cash-on-cash return requirement of potential equity investors. The required cash return on the equity investment is found by multiplying this return rate by the amount of equity invested.

Cash Equity Requirement × Cash-on-Cash Return Rate = Required Annual Cash Return

Net operating income (NOI) is the sum of the required annual cash return and debt service paid to the lender.

Required Annual Cash Return + Annual Debt Service = Net Operating Income (NOI)

Required market rent is found by adding expenses and vacancy losses to NOI to find gross potential revenue, and then dividing this figure by the number of units or square footage available for rent.

Net Operating Income (NOI) + Operating Expenses + Real Estate Taxes = Effective Gross Income

Effective Gross Income + Vacancy Allowance = Gross Potential Revenue

Gross Potential Revenue ÷ Rentable Units (or SF) = Required Rental Income per Unit (or SF)

Market-Driven Analysis Arithmetic

Market-driven analysis starts with market rent, which is multiplied by the amount of rental space available, to generate gross potential revenue.

Rentable Units (or SF) x Market Rent per Unit (or SF) = Gross Potential Revenue

Net operating income is found by deducting the cost of vacancies, operating expenses, and real estate taxes.

Gross Potential Revenue – Vacancy Allowance = Effective Gross Income

Effective Gross Income − (Operating Expenses + Real Estate Taxes) = Net Operating Income (NOI)

The amount of cash available for debt service is found by dividing the NOI by the required debt-service coverage ratio.

Net Operating Income (NOI) ÷ Debt-Service Coverage Ratio = Cash Available for Annual Debt Service

The difference between cash available for annual debt service and NOI is the amount available for distribution to equity investors, who have the residual claim on cash flows.

Net Operating Income (NOI) − Annual Debt Service = Cash Available for Investors

The justified equity investment is found by dividing this amount by the cash-on-cash return requirement. The justified mortgage amount is found by dividing annual debt service by the annualized mortgage constant.

Cash Available for Investors ÷ Cash-on-Cash Return Rate = Justified Equity Investment

Cash Available for Debt Service ÷ Annualized Mortgage Constant = Justified Mortgage Amount

The justified project investment is the sum of the justified equity investment and justified mortgage loan amounts.

Justified Equity Investment + Justified Mortgage Amount = Justified Project Investment

When hard and soft costs and site development costs are deducted from the justified project investment, the residual is the justified purchase price for the land.

Justified Project Investment − Anticipated Capital Improvement Budget = Justified Land Purchase Price

Clipper Mill, Baltimore, Maryland

DEVELOPER: Struever Bros. Eccles & Rouse

DESIGNER: Cho Benn Holback + Associates

WEBSITE: www.rosecompanies.com/all-projects/
clipper-mill-green-adaptive-re-use-of-historic-mill

Clipper Mill is an $88 million green, adaptive reuse of an historic mill on a 17.5-acre site in Baltimore, Maryland. Struever Bros. Eccles & Rouse developed this mixed use, transit-oriented project, converting 141,000 square feet of former foundry and mill buildings into offices, rental apartments, artists' studios, retail, and for-sale condos. Completed in 2006, Clipper Mill offers easy access by mass transit to retail and cultural destinations. A light-rail stop at the entrance to Clipper Mill links the community to a major shopping area, the University of Baltimore, and the Maryland Institute College of Art. A 14-mile bike-and-hiking trail system runs through the center of the community. The original mill and foundry were extensively damaged by fire in 1995; the architect retained the Assembly Building's fire-charred roof trusses while introducing new uses within the building shell. Winner of a 2008 Urban Land Institute Award for Excellence, Clipper Mill's location, adaptive reuse of existing buildings, and commitment to green building management practices have attracted a wide variety of tenants committed to sustainability. An affiliate of Jonathan Rose Companies is now the managing member of the ownership and continues to make green, energy-efficient improvements to the project.

Chapter 4

Apartment Project Alternatives

If a project-design sketch plan fails to meet the basic feasibility test, consider whether program alternatives will yield a better outcome. Taking the initial plan to the staff in the planning department for a preliminary review can identify possible alternative approaches under existing development regulations or new ones that may be applicable. The most promising alternatives can then be tested with further sketch plans and the application of cost-driven and market-driven analyses. Essentially, this is a process of asking: "What if we changed the program and site plan? Can we find ways to achieve higher design quality, financial returns, and community standards?"

Preliminary Review Alternatives: Asking "What If?"

Assume that the planning staff suggests investigating two alternatives during the preliminary review of the apartment project example we introduced in chapter 3. They point out that the recently revised zoning ordinance allows for two options that might increase the feasibility of the project:

1. An option to request rezoning of the site to a category that allows higher-density development, which should result in more compact, efficient land use
2. An option to follow new urbanism design standards that result in enhanced public spaces through placement of buildings and open space

The feasibility of these two options can be evaluated by making relatively straightforward revisions to the site plans and then running these revised plans through cost-driven and market-driven analyses using general categories of information that affect revenues and costs. At this stage, rule-of-thumb numbers are adequate to determine the relative feasibility of different alternatives.

If the preferred project proposal is refined further, then these rule-of-thumb assumptions would need to be modified to account for actual local construction and site costs, local market conditions, and other local realities. The number of possible options is limited only by the imagination of the developer and design team, and the willingness of local planners to provide input. Still, at the refinement stage, financial and time expenditures must be kept to manageable levels.

Changing the Zoning

In the illustrative case, a request to change the property to a higher-density multifamily zoning district could provide financial benefits for both the developer and the public. Under the existing zoning designation for the property, a maximum of eight apartment units to the gross acre is allowable. However, the zoning ordinance includes a second type of multifamily designation that allows for up to 16 units to the gross acre.

The design team determines that an additional 100 units can be accommodated by increasing the building heights to four stories on

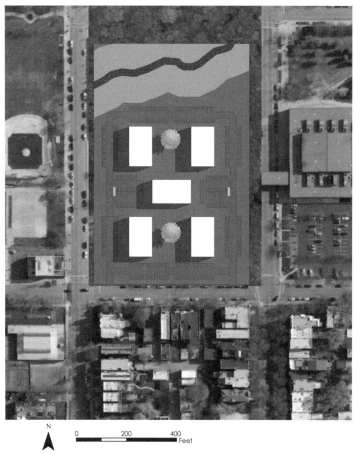

Figure 4-4. Apartment Project Rezoning: 200-Unit Alternative Plan

TABLE 4-1. APARTMENT PROJECT COST AND REVENUE ESTIMATES: REZONING CASE

INPUTS	BASE CASE	REZONING
Building in SF	130,500	261,000
Efficiency Ratio	0.91954	
Net Leasable Area in SF	120,000	240,000
Site in SF (Ac)	544,500 (12.5)	
Land Cost per SF	$2.50	
Land Cost	$1,361,250	
Site Development Costs, per Acre	$64,000	$96,000
Site Development Costs, Total	$800,000	$1,200,000
Hard Costs per SF	$119	$110
Soft Costs per SF at 20% of Hard Costs	$23.80	$22
Hard Costs	$15,529,500	$28,710,000
Soft Costs	$3,105,900	$5,742,000
Capital Budget without Land	$19,435,400	$35,652,000
Total Development Cost	$20,796,650	$37,013,250
Annualized Monthly Mortgage Constant	0.085972	
Loan-to-Cost Ratio	0.75	
Debt-Service Coverage Ratio	1.15	
Cash-on-Cash Return	0.12	
Operating Expenses per SF	$2.75	
Real Estate Taxes per $1,000	$12	
Rent per SF per Year	$18	
Other Income per SF per Year	$0.25	
Total Revenue per SF per Year	$18.25	
Vacancy Rate	0.05	
Unit Size in SF	1,200	1,200
Total Units	100	200

the same footprints and doubling the size of the parking areas. To explore this increased-density option, a sketch plan showing five four-story buildings of 40 units each is prepared (figure 4-4).

What are the cost and revenue implications of this zoning change? The ability to double the density of the development program greatly increases revenues. It also increases costs. Additional hard costs include the costs for the increased height of the buildings, the additional units, and the larger parking areas that are needed to serve the higher density. Additional soft costs include the preparation of the rezoning request and possibly the hiring of an attorney or other professionals to represent the developer in the governmental review process. Project risks are increased by the additional time it will take for the request to be reviewed, and the fact that the request may be denied. The inputs are shown in table 4-1.

TABLE 4-2. COST-DRIVEN ANALYSIS USING LOAN-TO-COST RATIO: REZONING CASE

COSTS	
Acquisition	$1,361,250
Hard Costs	$28,710,000
Soft Costs	$5,742,000
Site Development	$1,200,000
Total Development Cost	$37,013,250

EQUITY	
1 Minus Loan-to-Cost Ratio	0.25
× Cost	$37,013,250
= Equity Needed	$9,253,313
× Cash-on-Cash Return Rate	12%
= Required Cash Returns	$1,110,398

DEBT	
Total Development Cost	$37,013,250
× Loan-to-Cost Ratio	0.75
= Allowable Mortgage Amount	$27,759,938
× Annualized Monthly Mortgage Constant	0.0859720
= Annual Debt Service	$2,386,577

Debt-Service Coverage Ratio = 1.47

Cash Returns + Debt Service = NOI

Net Operating Income (NOI)	$3,496,975
+ Operating Expenses	$717,750
+ Real Estate Taxes	$444,159
= Effective Gross Income	$4,658,884
+ Vacancy	$245,204
= Gross Required Revenue	$4,904,088
÷ Net Leasable Area in SF	240,000
= Required Rental Income per SF	$20.43
Market Rent	$18.25
Required Rent / Market Rent	112%

TABLE 4-3. MARKET-DRIVEN ANALYSIS USING DEBT-SERVICE COVERAGE RATIO: REZONING CASE

Market Rent	$18.25
× Net Leasable Area in SF	240,000
= Gross Potential Revenue	$4,380,001
− Vacancy	$219,000
= Effective Gross Income	$4,161,001
− Operating Expenses	$717,750
− Real Estate Taxes	$444,159
Net Operating Income (NOI)	$2,999,092

EQUITY

Net Operating Income (NOI)	$2,999,092
− Debt Service	$2,607,906
= Cash Available for Investors	$391,186
÷ Cash-on-Cash Return Rate	12%
= Justified Equity Investment	$3,259,882

DEBT

Net Operating Income (NOI)	$2,999,092
÷ Debt-Service Coverage Ratio	1.15
= Cash Available for Debt Service	$2,607,906
÷ Annualized Monthly Mortgage Constant	0.0859720
= Justified Mortgage Amount	$30,334,363

Loan-to-Cost Ratio = 0.82

Equity Investment + Mortgage Amount = JPI

Justified Project Investment (JPI)	$33,594,246
− Total Development Cost without Land	$35,652,000
= Justified Land Purchase Price	$2,057,754
Land Cost	$1,361,250
Additional Funds Required	$3,419,004
Justified Investment / Total Development Cost	90.76%

The gross building area and net leasable area are doubled. The land cost stays the same, but site development costs increase by 50 percent, to $1.2 million, reflecting additional parking and site work. Hard costs and soft costs go down on a square-foot basis due to economies of size and scale. The total development cost of about $37 million for 200 units drives cost per unit down to $185,066 from $207,967 for 100 units. All other parameters remain the same as in the base case in chapter 3.

The cost and revenue implications are shown in tables 4-2 and 4-3. The estimated changes under the rezoning alternative are:

- Costs—Additional construction costs are incurred for increasing the five apartment buildings from two stories to four stories, and doubling the number of units and size of the parking areas. Hard costs per square foot are lower at larger scale with the same wood-frame construction type. Soft costs, estimated at 20 percent of hard costs, are higher because of the increased time and expense needed to pursue rezoning.
- Revenues—Increasing the number of units from 100 (8 per acre for 12.5 acres) to 200 (16 per acre for 12.5 acres) results in an expected gross potential revenue of $4.4 million.

As shown in the cost-driven analysis in table 4-2, the required rent is 12 percent over market rent. The market-driven analysis in table 4-3 shows that $3.4 million in additional funding is needed.

Clearly, increasing the density of the project through rezoning has positive impacts on financial feasibility. With 200 units, required rent is only 12 percent over market, compared to 24 percent in the base case. The shortfall of funding needed to complete the construction and purchase the land drops by almost $900,000, from $4.3 million in the base case. *Parcel assemblage*

Considering Alternate Ways to Meet Design Standards: Creating an Outdoor Room

Traditional zoning ordinances rely on two-dimensional standards, such as land use, lot size, density, setbacks, and open space require-

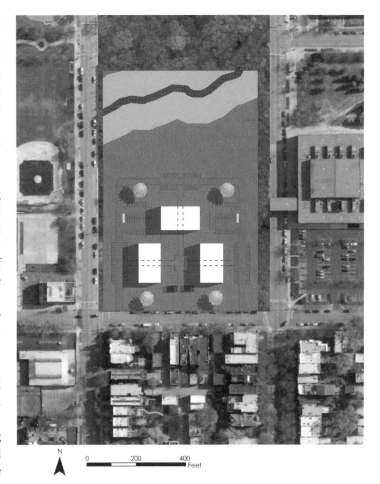

Figure 4-5. Apartment Project Design Standards: 120-Unit Plan with Commons.

ments. Such standards leave considerable leeway in the design of structures and public areas. The resulting appearance and functionality are often disappointing from both the public and private perspectives.

Contemporary development regulations may include building and site-design standards that go beyond traditional lists of allowable

Figure 4-6. Apartment Project Design Standards: 120-Unit Plan with Commons, Massing Study.

TABLE 4-4. APARTMENT PROJECT COST AND REVENUE ESTIMATES: DESIGN STANDARDS

INPUTS	BASE CASE	DESIGN STANDARDS
Building in SF	130,500	156,600
Efficiency Ratio	0.91954	
Net Leasable Area in SF	120,000	144,000
Site in SF (Ac)	544,500 (12.5)	
Land per SF	$2.50	
Land Cost	$1,361,250	
Site Development Costs, per Acre	$64,000	$32,000
Site Development Costs, Total	$800,000	$400,000
Hard Costs per SF	$119	$110
Soft Costs per SF at 20% of Hard Costs	$23.80	$22
Hard Costs	$15,529,500	$17,225,997
Soft Costs	$3,105,900	$3,445,199
Capital Budget without Land	$19,435,400	$21,071,196
Total Development Cost	$20,796,650	$22,432,446
Annualized Monthly Mortgage Constant	0.085972	
Loan-to-Cost Ratio	0.75	
Debt-Service Coverage Ratio	1.15	
Cash-on-Cash Return	0.12	
Operating Expenses per SF	$2.75	
Real Estate Taxes per $1,000	$12	
Rent per SF per Year	$18	$18
Other Income per SF per Year	$0.25	$0.75
Total Revenue per SF per Year	$18.25	$18.75
Vacancy Rate	0.05	
Unit Size in SF	1,200	1,200
Total Units	100	120

uses, setbacks, and open space requirements. They seek to create more complete three-dimensional environments in which the size, shape, height, and massing of the new structures are specified. The standards of these form-based codes are derived from participatory processes that involve the community in defining the appearance of future development (Elliott, Goebel, and Meadows 2012; Hall and Porterfield 2001). The standards may be required, or they may be optional with incentives, but they often include incentives of additional density and expedited development review if followed.

In the illustrative example, assume that the zoning ordinance includes an overlay provision that allows a 20 percent density bonus for designs that create an "outdoor room," defined as a public space that is formed by the location, height, and massing of adjacent buildings. Following this overlay provision would make it possible to add another 20 apartment units in return for redesigning the site plan to include such an outdoor room.

In order to create an outdoor room on the site, the designers reduce the number of buildings to three and increase the building heights to four stories. They group the three buildings to form three sides of an outdoor common area, with trellises defining the fourth side, and they open crosswalk passages to the commons through the ground floors. They place the parking behind the buildings in order to emphasize the sense of place engendered by the outdoor room. Figure 4-5 shows the plan in two dimensions. Figure 4-6 shows a three-dimensional massing study view of the design, with the buildings, rendered in SketchUp, overlaid on a Google view of the neighborhood. Only these basic design changes are considered in this simple illustration. More-elaborate form-based design moves could involve changes to the roof shapes, use of different materials, revisions to the building facades, addition of porches and balconies to add texture to the elevations, and so on.

Additional revenues from the rental of facilities are expected with the improved site plan and design; along with the additional amenities, that should result in more social interaction. The costs and revenues are summarized below and shown in table 4-4.

TABLE 4-5. COST-DRIVEN ANALYSIS USING LOAN-TO-COST RATIO: DESIGN STANDARDS

COSTS

Acquisition	$1,361,250
Hard Costs	$17,225,997
Soft Costs	$3,445,199
Site Development	$400,000
Total Development Cost	$22,432,446

EQUITY

1 Minus Loan-to-Cost Ratio	0.25
x Total Development Cost	$22,432,446
= Equity Needed	$5,608,112
x Cash-on-Cash Return Rate	12%
= Required Cash Returns	$$672,973

DEBT

Total Development Cost	$22,432,446
x Loan-to-Cost Ratio	0.75
= Allowable Mortgage Amount	$16,824,335
x Annualized Monthly Mortgage Constant	0.0859720
= Annual Debt Service	$1,446,422

Debt-Service Coverage Ratio = 1.47

Cash Returns + Debt Service = NOI

Net Operating Income (NOI)	$2,119,395
+ Operating Expenses	$430,650
+ Real Estate Taxes	$269,189
= Effective Gross Income	$2,819,234
+ Vacancy	$148,381
= Gross Required Revenue	$2,967,615
÷ Net Leasable Area in SF	144,000
= Required Rental Income per SF	$20.61
Market Rent	$18.25
Required Rent / Market Rent	110%

TABLE 4-6. MARKET-DRIVEN ANALYSIS USING DEBT-SERVICE COVERAGE RATIO: DESIGN STANDARDS

Market Rent	$18.75
× Net Leasable Area in SF	144,000
= Gross Potential Revenue	$2,700,000
− Vacancy	$135,000
= Effective Gross Income	$2,565,000
− Operating Expenses	$430,650
− Real Estate Taxes	$269,189
Net Operating Income (NOI)	$1,865,161

EQUITY

Net Operating Income (NOI)	$1,865,161
− Debt Service	$1,621,879
= Cash Available for Investors	$243,282
÷ Cash-on-Cash Return Rate	12%
= Justified Equity Investment	$2,027,349

DEBT

Net Operating Income (NOI)	$1,865,161
÷ Debt-Service Coverage Ratio	1.15
= Cash Available for Debt Service	$1,621,879
÷ Annualized Monthly Mortgage Constant	0.0859720
= Justified Mortgage Amount	$18,865,199

Loan-to-Cost Ratio = 0.84

Equity Investment + Mortgage Amount = JPI	
Justified Project Investment (JPI)	$20,892,548
− Total Development Cost without Land	$21,071,196
= Justified Land Purchase Price	$178,649
Land Cost	$1,361,250
Additional Funds Required	$1,539,899
Justified Investment / Total Development Cost	93.14%

Increases of 20 percent in gross and net building areas are consistent with the increase in total units from 100 to 120. As in the rezoning case, hard and soft costs are lower, and the reconfigured building arrangement halves site development costs to $400,000.

per unit basis →

The economic and financial implications of applying different design standards are shown in tables 4-5 and 4-6. The major changes are:

- Costs—Infrastructure costs (for streets, utilities, and so on) are reduced by 50 percent because less site clearing and grading is necessary. Expedited review reduces soft costs. Construction costs include three four-story buildings.
- Revenues—Additional revenues accrue from rents from 20 additional units, as well as increased other revenue from $0.25 to $0.75 per square foot.

As shown in table 4-5, the cost-driven analysis indicates that the required rent is 10 percent over market rent. The market-driven analysis in table 4-6 shows that additional funding in the amount of $1.5 million is required. The combination of cost savings from meeting the design standards and revenues from adding units makes this alternative better than the others.

This outcome is somewhat surprising. Doubling the project density is not more feasible than designing the buildings around an outdoor room at lower density. Based on this exploration of alternatives, the option of applying for approval under the design standards alternative is superior to both the base case and rezoning alternatives, as shown in table 4-7.

Further feasibility analysis of the design standards case would indicate the conditions under which this option would become financially feasible. For example, if market rent increased to $20 per square foot per year, the market-driven analysis would show that more than $1.7 million would remain to purchase the site, priced at $1.36 million, after funding all improvements. Rent increases of about 2.6 percent per year for

TABLE 4-7. COMPARISON OF APARTMENT ALTERNATIVES TO THE BASE CASE			
	BASE CASE (100 UNITS)	REZONING (200 UNITS)	DESIGN STANDARDS (120 UNITS)
Required Rent Over Market	124%	112%	110%
Additional Funds Required	$4,307,347	$3,419,004	$1,539,899

the subsequent three years would generate this rent level while the project was being approved, constructed, and leased. Conversely, if hard costs could be reduced by 10 percent, the project would become financially feasible even if rent remained at the current level. More-efficient design or construction techniques could lower hard costs. Development incentives offered by the local jurisdiction could reduce hard costs, soft costs, and acquisition costs, and consequently result in lower property taxes due to lower assessed value.

So far, our analysis has proceeded without consideration of development risk, an obviously important aspect of real estate development. We next discuss how risk can be understood in the context of the three alternative development schemes that have been analyzed.

Development Risk

Development risk is associated with each phase of the development process. Once the site is under the developer's control, idea refinement continues and feasibility analysis begins. The first major hurdle is receiving government approvals for the project. Developers call the risk of not receiving the rights needed to develop the property *entitlement risk*. The next major risk is associated with construction—site development, in particular—and it is termed *construction risk*. *Financial risk* pertains to both the availability of financing and its terms. *Market risk* arises from changes in supply-demand relationships and consumer tastes relative to competitive projects. *Lease-up risk* is often distinguished as a special form of market risk that pertains to the pace of space absorption after the certificate of occupancy is issued. During the refinement and feasibility stages, two forms of risk are relevant: market risk and entitlement risk. Financial, construction, and lease-up risks pertain to later stages of the development process.

When rezoning is pursued, entitlement risk increases from the base case because the probability of success is lower. Market risk is increased in two ways. Doubling the number of apartment units increases risk, because a larger number of units requires greater effort to lease and more time to absorb than a smaller number of units. Furthermore, the additional time required for rezoning pushes completion farther into the future, and conditions are more difficult to forecast as the time horizon lengthens.

The design standard alternative could lower entitlement risk by shortening the review process and by building goodwill in the community. Market risk is modestly higher in this case than in the base case but considerably lower than in the rezoning alternative. Market risk might also decline because the configuration of units may have more market appeal. These modifications would subsequently reduce construction risk by reducing the amount of land that is disturbed.

After considering all factors in this illustrative example, the development team would likely focus on the three-building 120-unit alternative in subsequent formal feasibility work. The incorporation of design standards that result in better design also positively affects the financial results due to the modest density increase that is allowed. The community is better served because this project will be more cost-effective to service, consume less land, and have broad community appeal.

The next step is to move into formal feasibility analysis.

Formal Feasibility Analysis

The developer generates an initial capital budget to nail down the cost side of the financial analysis. The task is to add detail to the four general cost categories used in the cost-driven and market-driven analyses: site acquisition, site development costs, hard costs, and soft costs.

Site Acquisition

The developer commissions an appraisal of the property to get an objective opinion of current market value. The appraisal of the property is also required by the permanent lender. The appraised value is expected to be equal to or greater than the option price the developer agrees to pay the landowner for the property. The appraiser needs information on the physical features of the site, the infrastructure available, the zoning in force, and so on. The appraiser usually pursues three approaches to valuation: historic cost, current market value, and future income potential. In finding the highest-and-best use of the site, the assessor considers the four dimensions: the use should be physically possible, legally allowed, economically productive, and financially feasible (see Appraisal Institute 2011). Although appraisers generally work independently, savvy developers put their appraiser in contact with the design team conducting the site analysis so they can share relevant information with one another. This interaction can improve the appraisal and generate insights useful to the design team.

Due diligence must be completed before the developer executes the option to purchase the site. The Phase I environmental study determines whether hazardous agents may be present on the site. If potential problems are detected, Phase II studies and Phase III remediation may be required. The developer's attorney conducts the title search to examine the property's chain of title. In the process, he or she may discover suspect uses of the site. The appraiser reviews this work before rendering an opinion of site value.

Site Development Costs

Accounting for site development costs is reasonably straightforward with the development program in place. That program establishes quality standards for the project that will be respected as design tasks are completed. Given these quality standards, the design team seeks to minimize land disturbance and infrastructure costs.

From the cost perspective, the total site acreage may be divided between developable areas and areas to be preserved. Areas to be preserved reflect difficult physical attributes of the site—such as severe topography, rocky or low-lying areas, or heavy vegetation—or regulatory requirements for open space, public easements, specimen trees, and, importantly, stormwater retention or detention.

Developable areas are used for ingress and egress, internal circulation, parking areas, and building pads. The associated horizontal land development includes costs for land disturbance, followed by infrastructure installation, and then landscaping. Estimates of the cost of site development for specific projects should rely on locally available cost information.

Hard Costs

Through interaction with the design team, the developer should be able to detail construction cost estimates. Several cost estimators are available for this purpose. RSMeans publishes information on construction costs in many different formats, and these are frequently used. Their publication *Square Foot Costs*, which is published annually and is also available online, provides estimates for residential, commercial, and civic buildings at the right level of detail for the feasibility stage.[1] In order to compare proposed designs, the developer can further refine hard-cost estimates by getting input from local general contractors.

The 2012 edition lists square-foot costs for apartments at three different scales, and details exactly how these figures were estimated. The factors considered are: square footage and linear footage of exterior walls; wood versus steel construction; and assumed features of the building, including substructure, shell, interiors, mechanical and electrical systems, and architect and contractor fees. Note that architect and contractor fees should be included in soft costs to avoid double counting.

Soft Costs

Soft costs are the costs of professional services and fees required to initiate construction. They include the expenses incurred to seek entitlements, assess the site, research the market, cover financing costs, raise equity, and establish the ownership structure. Soft costs also include the project contingency, developer's profit, insurance, and real estate taxes.

As the developer assembles the team, negotiates with lenders and investors, and takes the project through development review, he or she incurs most of these soft costs. They enter the capital budget as costs to be reimbursed instead of estimates of future financial obligations. Developers try to limit these predevelopment expenditures, also known as pursuit costs.

One very important soft cost is the estimate of construction-period interest. It depends on the amount of monthly draws of funds from the construction line of credit and the length of construction, both of which are difficult to estimate accurately during the project feasibility stage. A shortcut method is often used to generate this estimate. The length of the construction period, estimated in months, is divided into the total amount of the anticipated construction loan to get an average outstanding monthly balance. The monthly construction-period interest rate is then multiplied by the average outstanding monthly balance to get the monthly amount of construction interest owed. This amount is multiplied by the estimated months of construction to find total construction interest.

Another potential financing cost pertains to the construction loan. Construction lenders require their loans to be guaranteed. One of the equity investors may personally sign for the construction loan in return for a larger ownership share of the project. Otherwise, some other guarantee, such as a letter of credit, needs to be provided, the cost of which is added to soft costs.

Soft costs are largely known to the developer, locally determined, and project specific.

Real Estate Market Analysis

Formal market research is needed to estimate the revenue side of the preferred project more accurately. The developer usually wants to hire a market analyst to conduct an objective, arms-length study of the market and is usually required by the permanent lender to do so.

The market analysis for an apartment project involves forecasting demand for apartment units like the ones envisioned on the basis of employment projections for the area, forecasting supply on the basis of past building and business cycles, and comparing these forecasts. The market study shows whether the market is in balance, has excess supply, or has excess demand. The more detailed marketability study is conducted to determine a reasonable capture rate for the project and the time required to reach expected occupancy (monthly absorption schedule).

Real estate market analysis is a craft unto itself. When done carefully and accurately, it can generate the rent, vacancy, and expense estimates needed for credible discounted cash flow analysis. Basic references to consult are: Carn et al. (1988) and Fanning (2005).

market analysis ref.

Summary: Apartment Project Alternatives

As a game plan for development, the development program sets the strategy for the subsequent steps of development. However, the program is not written in stone at the start, but rather is a continuously evolving set of contingencies about the best way to accomplish the development goals. It changes during feasibility analysis as more information is obtained about the market, the regulatory climate, the physical site, and the financing terms and requirements.

One valuable way of testing the program contingencies is to ask "what if" they were changed in order to explore options beyond the original concept. Subjecting these alternatives to cost-driven and market-driven analyses allows them to be systematically compared to the base case. As shown in this chapter, the financial analysis need not be elaborate. Cost-driven and market-driven analyses will yield enough information to enable the developer and the designer to make the basic decision about whether or not to pursue the tested alternatives and which one looks most promising.

Once the development team has a promising alternative, more-detailed information about construction costs and market pros-

pects can be fleshed out through formal feasibility studies. This information is presented to the permanent lender and equity investors with the objective of getting their support for the project. Unlike real estate investment, where investors purchase property to receive cash flow from existing tenants, real estate development requires investors to buy a set of assumptions about the future embodied in the feasibility studies.

In this chapter, we compare the base case to two higher-density alternatives: a 200-unit alternative that requires rezoning, and a 120-unit project that emphasizes design standards. The 120-unit project turns out to be more attractive than either the base case or the rezoning alternative. An assessment of development risk also points to this alternative as the preferred one.

In balancing the trade-offs between project design, development feasibility, and regulatory standards, we find an attractive alternative. The project developer, the design team, and the community planners should embrace the final version of the design standards alternative. It should be favorably reviewed by the local jurisdiction and be the most formidable alternative for antidevelopment factions to defeat. When implemented, the project should contribute to local sustainable development.

From top to bottom: *Figure 5-1. Bradenton Village Housing (Courtesy of Cooper Johnson Smith Architects.); Figure 5-2. Bradenton Village Streetscape (Courtesy of Cooper Johnson Smith Architects.); Figure 5-3. Master Plan of Bradenton Village, Bradenton, Florida (Courtesy of Cooper Johnson Smith Architects.)*

Bradenton Village, Bradenton, Florida

DEVELOPER: Telesis Corporation

ARCHITECT: Cooper Johnson Smith Architects

WEBSITES: www.telesiscorp.com/projects/Bradenton/stats. htm; www.cjsarch.com/portfolio/bradenton-village-master-plan

Bradenton Village is a 39-acre redevelopment Traditional Neighborhood Development project in Bradenton, on the southwest Florida Gulf Coast. A new village green and a relocated community center make up the focus of this formerly distressed public housing project, which had been plagued with recurring floods prior to redevelopment. The project's village center serves the surrounding first-ring suburban neighborhoods with a child care center, library, and community center, while smaller neighborhood greens have smaller civic structures to meet residents' recreational needs. The master plan for this affordable housing community includes town houses, flats, and a community clubhouse and pool. The housing component is evenly split into market-rate, partially subsidized, and Section 8 housing. Developed by Telesis Corporation of Washington, D.C., in combination with the Bradenton Housing Authority, this HOPE VI–funded project won the Addison Mizner Medal for its village master plan, which includes 448 dwelling units, of which 338 are rental and 110 are in home ownership. This $75 million project was financed with $21.4 million in HOPE VI funds; a $250,000 grant from the City of Bradenton; and a combination of equity, grants, and private debt. Development rules came from both HUD program requirements and Bradenton zoning requirements.

Chapter 5

Residential Subdivision Alternatives

For more than 60 years, low-density residential development has been the dominant development type in the United States. Detached single-family housing has accounted for most of this development. The resulting decentralized suburban land-use pattern is found in all regions of the country. Even metro areas that had low growth or negative growth over the past 20 years continued to consume land in suburban areas for residential development. This pattern of sprawl development results in the inefficient provision of public facilities and services, negative environmental impacts, and excessive energy consumption (Bartholomew and Ewing 2009; Burton, Jenks, and Williams 2000). While it will not be possible to reverse the existing pattern in established suburban areas, it should be possible to increase the sustainability of future residential subdivision projects (Williamson 2013, Dunham-Jones and Williamson 2011).

Sustainable development alternatives seek to create residential subdivisions that use less land and energy and create fewer negative environmental impacts, while still meeting public health and safety standards and market demand. This chapter reviews the subdivision development process in order to explore the feasibility of creating more-sustainable subdivisions. It begins with an overview of the land development process and then lays out one form of feasibility analysis: revenue-expense analysis, which accounts for revenues and expenses in order to assess project solvency over time. We illustrate how it can be applied by using it to evaluate a conventional subdivision project and then comparing that base case with higher-density design alternatives.

The Land Development Process

Land development is the conversion of raw land or land used for agriculture or forestry into subdivided parcels of finished lots with services and amenities (Lamont 1979). Land developers undertake horizontal development: they purchase and subdivide the land, design and engineer the subdivision, seek public approvals, install infrastructure, and sell lots. Home builders buy finished lots from land developers and then do the vertical development, constructing houses on the finished lots. They build houses for specific households, known as custom-built homes, or they build on spec for the for-sale residential market. Major residential developers in the United States do both horizontal and vertical development, subdividing land and subsequently constructing houses.

Land developers use initial market research to gauge the growth forecast for households and how those households might be split between rental and home ownership. They associate the price range anticipated for the lots to a range of house prices. Typically about 20 to 25 percent of the total house price is spent on the lot. An estimate of the capture rate reflects both market depth and project risk. The capture rate is the percentage of home buyers in the price range who would need to buy units in the project in order for all the units to be sold.

Low Capture = Good

Low capture rates indicate deep markets and relatively low risk. High capture rates have the opposite implications.

If the market looks promising, land developers conduct several analyses to determine initial financial feasibility. First, static analysis of anticipated revenues for the lots, less development costs, would determine whether profit margins are adequate. In this analysis, revenues come from the sale of finished lots, and expenses are incurred for land purchase, project design and engineering, development reviews, site development, and carrying costs (interest paid on loans and other financing charges).

Land developers often seek equity investors. To attract potential investors, the discounted cash flow analysis needs to forecast expected returns in terms of before-tax internal rate of return (IRR). Simple cash-on-cash return calculations are also made. Investors provide equity when reasonable returns are anticipated. Because land development is one of the riskiest forms of real estate development, required returns have to be higher than returns on apartments, office, retail, or other income-generating or commercial properties.

more Risk in Land Dev.

After completing the initial examination of the physical, legal and planning, economic, and financial dimensions, the land developer begins more-detailed dynamic analysis. The most basic financial feasibility question pertains to *solvency*. Can the land developer maintain a positive cash position from the time of initial expenditures to the completion of lot sales? This question is important for anyone involved in a real estate development, but it is especially important for land developers. As the amount of land under control increases, achieving solvency becomes more challenging. Indeed, large-scale land developments, including new towns such as Reston, Virginia, have sometimes sent the original land developer into bankruptcy or foreclosure, while others faced major long-term challenges (Reston Town Center Association 2013; Forsyth 2005).

Risk Management

Land development is the riskiest form of real estate development because up-front investment is required to gain control of the site and construct infrastructure before any returns from lot sales can be realized. Land developers use several approaches to manage risk. The most important one is the two-party contract.

The land developer or buyer uses the offer-to-purchase agreement and the sales/purchase contract, and makes a payment of earnest money to secure site control. These documents spell out conditions and terms that govern the due diligence examination of the site and each party's responsibilities.

explain

The land developer often secures seller financing—in the form of a purchase-money mortgage or note—as an early-stage and relatively inexpensive source of funds. The parcel provides the collateral for this loan, and release provisions are carefully specified. The land developer may also be able to secure a land development loan from a construction lender. The loan-to-cost ratio is historically in the 30–50 percent range. This is low compared to loan-to-cost ratios in other forms of real estate development and is another indication of the risks associated with land development. The land and infrastructure improvements provide the lender's security, and the loan agreement explains how parcels will be released from the land seller to the lender and eventually to the home builders. The developer will ask the seller to subordinate his or her priority to collect on the debt to that of the lender, who then acquires the first lien on the property. Sellers are motivated to subordinate in order to defer taxes on the capital gains incurred in the land transaction.

With each investor, the land developer has a two-party contract that covers the amount and timing of cash infusions, the return on capital, and the return of capital. To induce investors to participate, they are often put in a preferred position to receive cash before the developer. The land development loan requires a guarantee, which is often provided by one investor in return for a greater ownership share. The developer who is able to offer a letter of credit instead can retain that share.

The land developer enters into a two-party contract with the general contractor who will manage site development and the installation of infrastructure. The general contractor has contracts with subcontractors who do the work. As a risk-control technique, the land developer normally holds back some payment for work done until site development is completed. Land developers shoulder less risk in getting the site developed if the land development loan is structured flexibly as a revolving line of credit rather than being tied directly to lot release and specific improvements. With this flexibility, it is easier for the general contractor and, in turn, the subcontractors to be paid as needed.

Finally, the land developer has contracts with home builders who will purchase lots and do the house construction. The number and timing of lot sales are specified, as well as the financing terms, because builders often are not well enough capitalized to purchase lots outright. (See Peiser and Hamilton 2012, chapter 3, for a detailed discussion of land development.)

Solvency Analysis

Solvency analysis is important because the expenses to develop land are incurred months before revenues from the sale of finished lots are realized. These expenses are financed from two major sources: 1) equity provided by the land developer and investors, and 2) debt provided through land development (construction) financing and possibly landowner financing (purchase-money mortgage or note). Funds are used to purchase the land, design the subdivision, pay the costs of going through the development review process, generate the engineering drawings for the infrastructure, develop the site (undertake grading and erosion control, and install water and sewers, roads and circulation, and amenities), and market lots to home builders. The project first must achieve solvency by maintaining a positive cash position over time—that is, cash in must be greater than cash out. Then the land developer can focus on making more-detailed estimates of the project's potential profitability. Solvency analysis determines whether the land developer can stay cash positive from the time money is first spent through the time lot sales begin. The land development period ends when lot sales to home builders repay the construction and any other outstanding loans.

Two basic forecasts frame the solvency analysis. Revenues depend on the *absorption schedule*, which shows the number of lots that

the developer can expect to sell each month after land development is completed. The land developer also needs a good forecast of the *timing of expenses*, which aggregates the funds needed to gain site control, design and engineer the project, complete the development reviews, secure the financing, and develop the site. These forecasts are brought together in the development timeline.

The key tools of solvency analysis, then, are the *development timeline* and the associated *revenue-expense analysis*. The timeline, which is discussed next, specifies the tasks that need to be completed as the project is developed. The revenue-expense analysis accounts for the expected monthly cash flows throughout the development period, in order to show how much funding the developer needs so as not to run out of money before the project is completed. In practice, enough time needs to be devoted to data collection to make the results credible, but achieving high levels of precision is usually not worth the effort at this stage in the development process. The revenue-expense analysis is presented for an illustrative base case of a greenfield subdivision and alternative subdivision plans for the property.

Land Development Timeline

The land development timeline shown in figure 5-4 involves five major tasks and spans 36 months. For subdivisions of more than 10 parcels, the time needed to accomplish these tasks in most jurisdictions would be considerably longer, perhaps 4–5 years. The time needed to complete larger planned unit developments would be 5–10 years. Large parcels are developed in phases as a way to generate lot sales as soon as feasible and reduce development risk. The timeline here is long enough to illustrate the technique but very optimistic as an actual development scenario.

The major tasks are: 1) gaining control of a viable site, 2) designing and engineering the project to gain public approvals, 3) developing the site, and 4) marketing and selling the finished lots to home builders. Financing is the fifth on-going task, and it provides the funds needed to execute the first three tasks before revenues can be generated through lot sales.

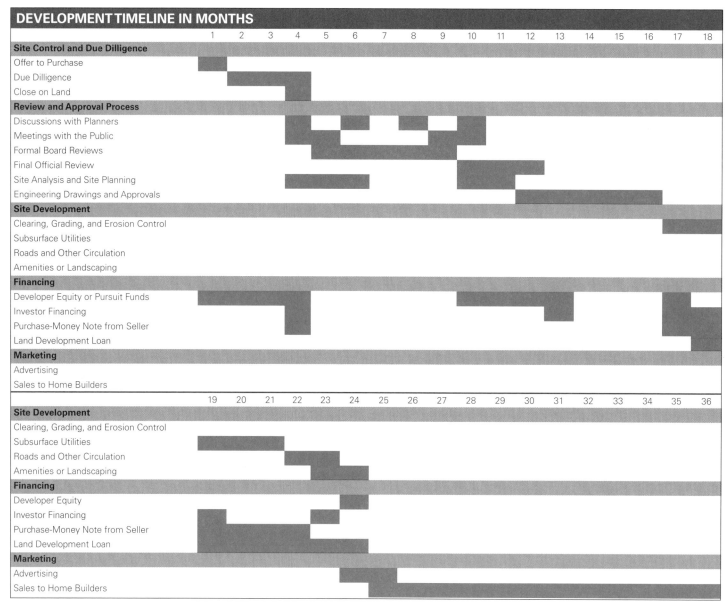

Figure 5-4. Development Timeline

Site control and due diligence begin when the landowner accepts the developer's offer to purchase. Due diligence occurs for the next three months. The developer purchases the land in the fourth month. In many cases, the developer may not have to close on the land before the project receives public approvals. If the landowner agrees to wait until entitlements are granted, the price for the land will reflect the added time and risk involved.

Land developers often use options to gain site control in order to defer land purchase. In this illustration, the developer gives the land-owner a down payment and secures a purchase-money note for the balance.

Due diligence is specified in the purchase agreement. The land developer investigates the four dimensions in sufficient detail to move forward. The Phase I environmental assessment and preliminary analysis of site conditions (such as topography or wetlands) address the physical dimension. The title search and reviews of tax assessment records, existing zoning, and other regulations cover the legal dimension. Together these dimensions define the development envelope of the site. Initial market analysis deals with current and prospective economic conditions. The financial analysis estimates the maximum land price given the development envelope and market conditions, as well as assessing returns.

Project review and approvals can be a lengthy process, usually more than the eight months shown in the timeline in figure 5-4. This process involves discussions with planners and city staff, multiple meetings with citizens and concerned neighbors, formal presentations before regulatory advisory boards, and final reviews by elected officials. To conduct the site analysis and formulate the site plan, the developer works with a land planner usually trained in landscape architecture. The developer works with an engineer to design the infrastructure—water lines, sanitary and storm sewers, roads and other improvements in the rights-of-way, and any amenities to be provided, such as greenways and recreation areas. After city officials approve the site plan, the city engineer is usually responsible for subsequent approval of the engineering drawings.

The site plan and engineering drawings are implemented during site development, which takes eight months for the illustrative subdivision. This time frame is feasible if site development begins in a timely manner so as to avoid adverse weather conditions. For instance, in the southeast, it would be considered very good timing to initiate site development early in the calendar year so that the road beds and poured surfaces are installed before the end of August. Adverse weather, including hurricanes, often begins to occur in September.

Like home builders, who need certificates of occupancy before house closings can occur, the land developer needs professional city staff to certify completion of the subdivision. Often it is preferable to defer making the final touches until houses are built. Typically, in order to begin releasing lots to home builders as soon as possible, the land developer will want to record the plat as soon as street paving is finished. The developer provides a completion bond to the jurisdiction to insure that the landscaping, amenities, and final features will be installed later.

Although home builders market the lots and pay broker commissions, the land developer usually assists in facilitating lot sales. In this example, 12 months are needed to sell all of the lots. A typical absorption schedule for a successful medium-size project would have at least half of the lots sold to home builders in the first three months. There would then be a lull in sales while the home builders used their inventory, followed by the sale of the remaining lots in the last three months of the period.

Revenue-expense analyses associated with this timeline are discussed below for each of the subdivision alternatives. For these site plans, a local development company and engineering firm familiar with this site provided the site development estimates. Usually, qualified designers and engineers have the local knowledge needed to estimate site-specific costs. Local cost data that pertain to the jurisdiction are also needed to illustrate the logic of revenue-expense analysis. These costs vary widely from place to place. For example, impact fees are high in California and Florida but nonexistent in many southeastern states. Some jurisdictions expect detailed impact analyses like those noted in chapter 2, which can cost hundreds of thousands of dollars. Other jurisdictions require very little work on impacts. Fees for applications and permits vary widely. Legal costs depend on how long and contentious the development review is. Except for the site development costs and design and engineering charges, the other expense estimates shown below are ballpark figures.

Illustrative Case: Residential Subdivision

For purposes of illustration, assume that a land developer is considering developing a medium-size residential subdivision in a growing suburban area. Developments of this scale and type are common. They will not reverse the trend of suburban sprawl, but they can improve the density, affordability, and walkability of the average subdivision.

In this illustrative case, the land developer has located a 36-acre parcel of property that is on the market. The property is adjacent to an existing 95-acre subdivision of single-family houses and townhomes developed in the 1990s, and is served by public water and sewer. Access is provided by an existing highway along the west border and a stub-out street from the adjacent subdivision on the east side. The land is relatively flat, falling off to a small lake to the south. A high-tension power line easement traverses the site from northeast to southwest (shown with pole locations in figure 5-5).

The question for the development team is whether residential development on this parcel is feasible. To answer that question, the developer and design team look at the constraints and incentives provided in the local development ordinance in terms of allowable density, lot sizes, setbacks, open space set-asides, and other subdivision approval requirements.

The designers then conduct a site analysis and develop programs and concept plans that are subjected to various feasibility analyses. As part of the site analysis, base conditions—including the site's topography, slope, vegetation, waterways, roads, and utilities—are mapped and evaluated in order to generate a map of development

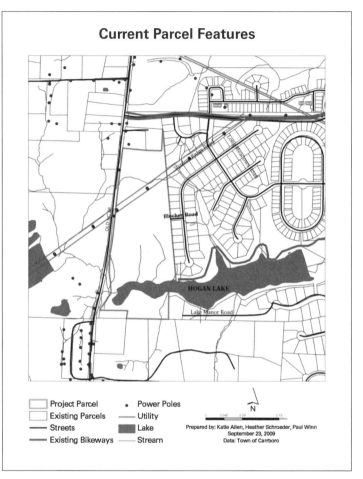

Figure 5-5. Site Location and Parcel Features: Potential Residential Subdivision (Site analysis by Katie Allen, Heather Schroeder, and Paul Winn, 2009. Used by permission.)

opportunities and constraints. Development programs test various combinations of subdivision plans that can be developed under ordinance requirements. Design concept plans are then prepared in order to show how roads, lots, and utilities may be arranged on the site; the resulting number of lots that can be created; and the estimated costs of overall development. Finally, each alternative concept is analyzed for its economic and financial implications.

Development Regulation Options

The development ordinance in this illustrative case is based on the Land Use Ordinance of Carrboro, North Carolina (Town of Carrboro 2009). The ordinance requires that residential developments provide sufficient active recreation areas and facilities based on the number and type of residential dwellings in the subdivision. The proposed development must earn a minimum of recreational points based on the provision of recreation amenities and must maintain at least 40 percent of the parcel as open space.

Under the land-use ordinance, the property is zoned R-20, which requires a minimum lot size of 20,000 square feet and permits single-family, two-family, and multifamily residences, various public and semipublic facilities, and recreational facilities. The maximum allowable number of lots is computed by dividing the size of the parcel in acres by the minimum lot size of 20,000 square feet. In this case, the allowable number of lots is 78 (36 acres × 43,560 square feet ÷ 20,000 square feet). However, the ordinance gives incentives in the form of flexible lot sizes and additional density to accomplish public objectives such as provision of affordable housing and conservation of open space and environmental resources.

The Affordable Housing Density Bonus allows the maximum density to be increased by two dwelling units for every one affordable housing unit, up to a maximum of 120 percent of the allowable density. The bonus is available if at least 15 percent of the housing units are affordable. Under this provision, open space may be reduced by an amount equal to twice the area of the affordable housing lots, although it cannot be less than 20 percent of the total site area. Minimum lot width is 100 feet, and buildings must be set back from the street right-of-way line by 40 feet and from the lot boundary by 20 feet.

Density bonus explained

The Architecturally Integrated Subdivision guidelines allow buildings to be built without regard to minimum lot size or setback re-

strictions, although overall site density may not exceed 20,000 square feet per acre. Lots must be of sufficient size to support the proposed structures, and lots on the subdivision border must still meet setback requirements. The land saved by creating smaller lots must be set aside as open space.

The Cluster Subdivision guidelines allow lot sizes to be reduced in order to preserve open space. However, in this case the cluster lots in an R-20 zone must still be a minimum of 15,000 square feet in size, and the land saved must be set aside as open space. The minimum lot size provision makes this option less desirable than the Architecturally Integrated Subdivision alternative.

Site Analysis

The land-use ordinance requires that development avoid Primary Conservation Areas containing steep slopes, defined as those greater than 25 percent; limit development in Secondary Conservation Areas containing moderate slopes of 15 to 25 percent; and concentrate development in areas with suitable slopes of 0 to 15 percent. It defines open areas and pine forests as suitable for development, mixed woodlands as moderately suitable (Secondary Conservation Areas), and hardwood areas as unsuitable (Primary Conservation Areas). Development is prohibited in wetland areas and within a 60-foot buffer around lakes and streams.

The resulting map of areas suitable for development shows the impact of various constraints on the potential of the site for subdivision. The lake and its buffer are protected from development. A few areas of hardwood trees and moderate slopes constrain development, but most of the site is suitable for development. (See figure 5-6.)

Development Proposal Program

The first development scheme (base case) makes use of the Architecturally Integrated Subdivision allowances in order to reduce the lot sizes to make better use of the property. The proposed subdivision includes single-family dwellings on 59 lots, along with recreation space. The proposed development maintains more than the required 40 per-

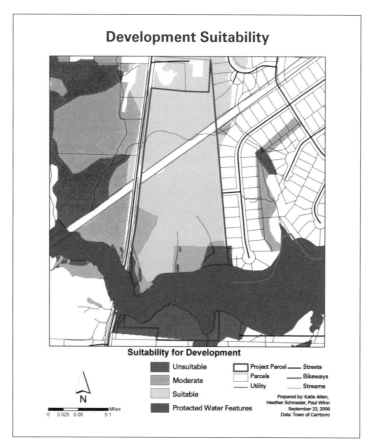

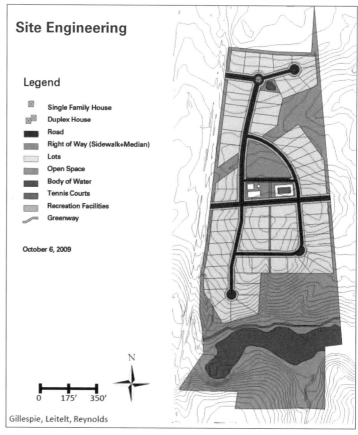

Figure 5-6 (left). Development Suitability Analysis (Site analysis by Katie Allen, Heather Schroeder, and Paul Winn, 2009. Used by permission.)

Figure 5-7 (right). Subdivision Base Case Concept Plan (Subdivision concept plan by Erin Gillespie, Lyle Leitelt, and Sara Reynolds, 2009. Used with permission.)

cent of the 36-acre parcel (14.5 acres) as open space. The recreational amenities include a greenway, gazebo, playground, tennis court, and basketball court.

Base Case Concept Plan
The development plan is designed to incorporate multiple environmental constraints: existing infrastructure, hydrology, slopes, soil,

and vegetation. All proposed structures are located on land with suitable slopes and soil, outside of utility easements, and away from existing hardwood trees. Open space is concentrated around the lake and the recreation area in the center of the site.

External automobile circulation is designed around an east-west street linking a stub-out connection from the adjacent subdivision on the east to the existing highway on the west, as well as another connection to the road on the west at the northern end of the site. Internal circulation provides access to lots and to the recreation area with a pool and tennis court and open space at the heart of the neighborhood. Lots, which vary in size and shape, average around 12,000 square feet. Pedestrian circulation is oriented to a north-south greenway, which connects the open spaces inside the project with one another and with the lake, while a new east-west greenway connects with the existing greenway in the adjacent subdivision to the east. (See figure 5-7.)

Base Case Financial Analysis

The financial analysis for the base case roughly follows the development timeline in figure 5-4. In the financial statement shown in table 5-1, the sources and uses of funds are presented for this case. The land developer begins the analysis with this static statement to gauge the amount of funding needed to cover expenses and the extent to which revenues exceed expenses. The net positive cash position looks promising.

The developer will use revenues from lot sales to repay the land development loan and the purchase-money note. The amount repaid for the loan is $1.214 million, which includes the interest expense. The deal with the landowner involves payment of $990,000 in two monthly installments when lot sales are realized. The extra $90,000 is the return to the landowner for providing seller financing. The return is 10 percent for lending $900,000 for eight months, or about 13 percent annualized.

Table 5-2 presents the revenue-expense analysis for the base case covering 36 months. The land developer can achieve solvency (zero or net positive cash flow throughout the period) by finding sufficient funding to pay for developing the site. In the base case, solvency depends on the developer's ability to raise $1.84 million in equity for the project.

The land developer expects to cover the expenses incurred for the first two phases of the project, until entitlements are granted in the 12th month. The exception is the remaining down payment on the land, which an investor covers in the fourth month. The next

TABLE 5-1. USES AND SOURCES OF FUNDS FOR LAND DEVELOPMENT: SUBDIVISION BASE CASE

USES		SOURCES	
Land	$1,200,000	Land Development Loan	$1,214,000
Site Development	$1,905,000	Purchase-Money Note	$900,000
Design and Engineering	$290,000	Investor Equity	$1,195,000
Permits, Fees, Other	$530,000	Developer Equity	$642,000
Financing Costs	$26,000	Total Sources	$3,951,000
Total Uses/Expenses	$3,951,000	Revenues from Lot Sales	$4,720,000
Estimates were provided by Jim Earnhardt, Bryan Properties, Inc.; Chad Blackmon, Blackmon Development Associates, PLLC; and the authors.			

four months are needed to get the engineering analysis and related drawings completed. In month 17, the engineer is paid, the purchase-money note is executed to move ownership of the site to the developer and investors, and site work begins. The investors begin to finance the project and are the only source of funds for the next two months.

The land development loan is closed in month 18, but it is not tapped until the 20th month, to minimize interest expenses. The loan is structured as a revolving line of credit (as are most construction loans) at 4 percent annual interest, which is variable and charged monthly at 0.33 percent. The loan is limited to about $1.2 million, plus interest expense, which represents a loan-to-cost ratio of about 30 percent ($1.2 million loan divided by total expenses).

The site is developed in eight months. Two months are allocated for site preparation, three months for installation of infrastructure, two months for the construction of roads and other circulation, and one month to finish the amenities.

The project is completed in 24 months. The land development loan and subordinated purchase-money note cover $2.11 million, or 54 percent of total financing sources. Equity from the developer and investors covers the other 46 percent of the $3.95 million total. Without seller financing, the developer would have had to raise 69 percent of the funds, or $2.74 million.

TABLE 5-2. REVENUE-EXPENSE ANALYSIS: SUBDIVISION BASE CASE

BASE CASE	MONTHS											
	1	2	3	4	5	6	7	8	9	10	11	12
Site Control and Due Diligence												
Earnest Money Deposit	$50,000											
Down Payment to Landowner				$250,000								
Pursuit / Due Diligence Costs		$40,000	$40,000									
Review and Approval Process												
Application Fees and Permits				$160,000								
Land Planning / Design				$20,000								$30,000
Impact Studies, Public Relations										$150,000		
Engineering Analysis and Drawings												$80,000
	$50,000	$40,000	$40,000	$430,000						$150,000		$110,000
Financing												
Developer's Equity Investment	$50,000	$40,000	$40,000	$180,000						$150,000		$110,000
Investor's Equity Investment				$250,000								

	MONTHS											
	13	14	15	16	17	18	19	20	21	22	23	24
Site Development and Land												
Balance Due to Engineer					$160,000							
Balance Due to Landowner					$900,000							
Site Preparation and Erosion Control					$140,000	$150,000						
Soft Costs (Insurance, Taxes)												$130,000
Infrastructure Installation							$315,000	$300,000	$300,000			
Roads and Circulation										$300,000	$225,000	
Amenities											$75,000	$100,000

TABLE 5-2. REVENUE-EXPENSE ANALYSIS: SUBDIVISION BASE CASE

	MONTHS											
	13	14	15	16	17	18	19	20	21	22	23	24
Financing Costs												
Development Loan Fee						$12,000						
Interest on Land Development Loan								$1,000	$2,000	$3,000	$3,670	$4,000
Marketing Costs												
Advertising												$10,000
					$1,200,000	$162,000	$315,000	$301,000	$302,000	$303,000	$303,670	$244,000
Financing												
Developer's Equity Investment						$12,000						$60,000
Investors' Equity Investment					$300,000	$150,000	$315,000				$100,000	$80,000
Purchase-Money Note					$900,000							
Land Development Loan Draws								$301,000	$302,000	$303,000	$203,670	$104,000
					$1,200,000	$162,000	$315,000	$301,000	$302,000	$303,000	$303,670	$244,000

	MONTHS											
	25	26	27	28	29	30	31	32	33	34	35	36
Financing Repayments												
Purchase-Money Note Repayment		$600,000	$390,000									
Interest on Land Development Loan		$14,000										
Land Development Loan Repayment	$1,100,000	$100,000										
	$1,100,000	$714,000	$390,000									
Marketing Revenues												
Lot Sales to Home Builders	$1,200,000	$800,000	$400,000							$960,000	$960,000	$400,000
Net Cash Flow	$100,000	$86,000	$10,000							$960,000	$960,000	$400,000
Cumulative Cash Flow	$100,000	$186,000	$196,000	$196,000	$196,000	$196,000	$196,000	$196,000	$196,000	$1,156,000	$2,116,000	$2,516,000

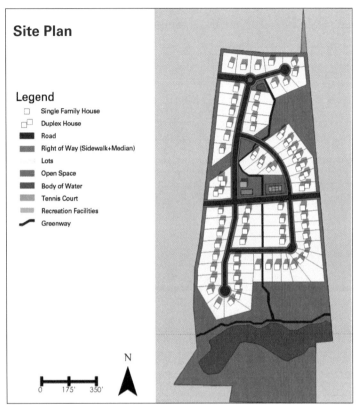

Figure 5-8. Subdivision with Affordable Housing Units (Adapted from site plan prepared by Erin Gillespie, Lyle Leitelt, and Sara Reynolds, 2009. Used with permission.)

Revenues from lot sales begin in the 25th month. For the first three months, most of the proceeds are used to repay the land development loan and the seller. Substantial positive net cash flows are not realized until the last three months of the period. The cash-on-cash return to developer and investors is 37 percent ($679,000 divided by $1.837 million). Although this amount appears to be a very handsome return, three points should be kept in mind: First, the actual return on present-value basis is lower due to the time value of money, the concept that having money today is worth more than having the same amount of money in the future. Second, the developer and investors commit $820,000 in the first year of the project, almost two years before any returns are realized. Third, the solvency analysis is based on the expected scenario. The developer takes on all of the risk of delays, added costs, and slower lot sales. As noted earlier, land development is the riskiest form of real estate development, and returns need to be sufficiently high to reflect this risk.

As noted on the timeline in figure 5-4, the land developer begins to meet with the local planners in the fourth month, when site control is secured. Initial informal discussions with the planners, neighborhood representatives from the adjoining subdivision, and other local developers make it clear that the project's chances of being approved will be enhanced significantly if affordable housing units are included.

Alternative Subdivision Adding Affordable Housing Bonus

In order to test the feasibility of applying the Affordable Housing Density Bonus, the base case layout is amended to add 12 affordable duplex lots, each containing two affordable housing units, reducing the number of single-family lots from 59 in the base case to 53. This results in a new design density of 77 units: 53 single-family units and 24 affordable units in 12 duplex buildings.

Under the Architecturally Integrated Subdivision, density can be increased to up to 120 percent of the original, resulting in a new maximum allowable number of 93 units (78 × 120 percent). However, the additional density is not needed, because even with the additional duplex units and single-family lots, the new density of 77 units is below the original allowable density of 78 units. The constraint on this site, as is often the case, comes from the requirement to maintain 40 percent open space, in combination with site features such as the power line easement, slopes, and tree preservation area.

The design logic of this alternative scheme is to maintain the original road layout but to place the new higher-density duplex lots adjacent to the large central open space. As a result, these new duplex

Figure 5-9. Subdivision in Context with Adjacent Neighborhood (Site plan overlaid on GIS map by the authors.)

units are within easy walking distance of the central recreation area with its pool and tennis court (see figure 5-8).

A potential benefit of the affordable housing alternative is its appeal to the local government because it increases the equity of the housing supply, which could increase the likelihood of approval. However, there is also the possibility of opposition to the affordable housing from residents of the existing neighborhood. Physically, the proposed project fits into the local context quite well, basically extending to the west the residential development pattern of the exist-

ing neighborhood on the east, where larger lot sizes average about 12,000 square feet and smaller lots average about 6,000 square feet (see figure 5-9).

Affordable Housing Financial Analysis

Adding affordable units has minimal impact on the expense side of the project. The cost of infrastructure installation and roads increases by about $90,000 for the six additional lots. Investors cover this additional amount.

The major impact is on revenues from lot sales. On the positive side, this alternative increases the total number of lots to be sold from 59 in the base case to 65. However, the price of lots is less on average. The 12 lots devoted to 24 affordable units are priced at $40,000 each. Lots in the northern portion of the site and at the southern end are priced at $80,000, the same as in the base case. However, 13 lots in the center of the site and close to the duplexes are priced at $60,000 on average. This outcome reflects the market as perceived by the home builders who will be bidding on and buying the lots. They envision building smaller single-family units near the duplexes to achieve more consistency and compatibility among the housing types and more variety overall.

The cumulative net cash flow is $2.26 million, which is $260,000 less than in the base case. This amount divided by equity, which is $90,000 higher than in the base case, reduces the cash-on-cash return rate to about 17 percent ($329,000 divided by $1.927 million). The land developer and particularly the investors are not impressed with this outcome. The developer decides to meet again with the design team to come up with a new approach to the site. The best-case outcome would generate a physical design more appealing to the market, the neighbors, and the locality, and one that increases returns closer to the 37 percent level achieved in the base case.

Alternative Programming Strategy

After reviewing the site analysis and development objectives, the development team decides to explore an additional alternative that will keep the 65-parcel site plan but with several important modifications.

This involves several new programming assumptions:

- The project is conceived as a green community. Arrangements are made with the power company for it to purchase electricity produced by solar collectors on the new houses.
- The county extension service agrees to establish a community garden in the rear portion of the right-of-way and teach interested residents techniques for organic farming, such as raised beds, sequential planting, drip irrigation, and pest control.
- The public transit agency agrees to extend service to the area during morning and evening hours, connecting it to the town center, employment concentrations, and shopping areas.
- The number of parcels devoted to affordable units is reduced from 12 to 10, which still satisfies the 15 percent affordable housing requirement.
- The two formerly affordable duplexes near the entrance of the site are converted to market-rate duplexes.
- The four lots south of the main entry road are to be marketed for duplexes or town houses.
- The tennis court and pool are eliminated, and the open space in the center of the site is programmed for passive recreation. This assumes that the developer will be able to negotiate an agreement with the adjacent neighborhood home owners association by which households from the new area can become members and use their facilities. These include active play areas for children, a swimming pool with associated facilities, areas for group meals or meetings, and several tennis courts.

Alternative Programming Financial Analysis

The programming changes positively affect financial returns. The savings from the reduction of amenities plus the free advertising achieved through establishing the community garden and county extension courses saves the developer $90,000, which compensates for the added costs of the six lots. The new product mix retains the $80,000 target price for the 49 lots programmed for single-family houses. The 10 lots for affordable duplexes are to be sold for $40,000 each, as in the previous case. The six lots for market-rate duplexes or town houses are priced from $60,000 to $70,000, with the lower price assumed in the analysis.

The cumulative net cash flow from this alternative is $2.48 million after the loans are repaid, only $40,000 less than in the base case. The profit is the difference between this amount and invested equity. The profit divided by invested equity generates a cash-on-cash return rate of 34.8 percent ($639,000 divided by $1.837 million). The land developer and investors find this outcome attractive, assuming that the modifications are acceptable under the local government zoning ordinance. This alternative offers an appealing physical design, more marketable product mix, more on-site and adjacent amenities, affordable housing units, and fewer adverse environmental impacts.

The analyses of an affordable housing alternative and an alternative programming strategy illustrate the potential impact of regulatory flexibility in determining the framing of development proposals. Chapter 7 looks at the impact of addressing neighborhood concerns in the design of a complex infill redevelopment project.

Summary: Residential Subdivision Alternatives

This chapter explores the feasibility of creating more-sustainable residential subdivisions. We describe the land development process from the developer's perspective, the associated risks, and the ways developers manage risk. The critical financial criterion is project solvency, the ability to maintain a net positive cash flow over time. The land development timeline feeds into the revenue-expense analysis, which is used to keep track of all cash inflows and outflows needed over the development period.

We apply revenue-expense analysis to evaluate a conventional 36-acre subdivision project. The site plan shows undeveloped areas, internal circulation, a recreation facility, associated open space, a greenway, and 59 finished lots. The land developer needs $3.95 million to complete the project in 24 months and then hopes to sell the lots to home builders over the next 12 months for $4.72 million. Financial returns are attractive.

The development team decides that affordable units are needed as part of the proposed subdivision to increase the chances of favorable public review. Although the revised site plan increases density, the financial returns drop sufficiently to make the project unattractive given the inherent land development risks. The team comes up with another alternative that brands the project as a green community and makes numerous modifications. As a result, financial returns rebound, almost to the same level as in the original site plan; the good subdivision layout is maintained; and significant public benefits are added to the project. The team expects the project to be favorably reviewed and approved.

Belmar, Lakewood, Colorado

DEVELOPERS: Continuum Partners, LLC; McStain Neighborhoods; Trammell Crow Residential

DESIGNERS: Van Meter Williams Pollack Denver; QPK Design, Shears Adkins Architects, LLC; Belzberg Architects; Civitas, Inc.; EDAW, Inc.; Elkus Manfredi Architects

PUBLIC PARTNERS: City of Lakewood, Lakewood Reinvestment Authority

WEBSITE: www.belmarcolorado.com

From top to bottom: Figure 6-1. Belmar Skating Rink (Courtesy of Belmar, Lakewood, Colorado.); Figure 6-2. Belmar Mixed Use Building (Courtesy of Belmar, Lakewood, Colorado.); Figure 6-3. Site Plan, Center of Belmar, Lakewood, Colorado (Courtesy of Elkus Manfredi Architects.)

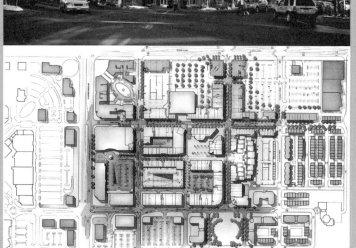

Belmar shows how an aging bedroom-suburb corridor within Lakewood, an inner suburb adjacent to Denver, can become a more diverse, compact, sustainable, and pedestrian- and transit-oriented place. Its staged redevelopment includes retail, office, multifamily, and other commercial uses. At build-out, this 22-block area will serve as Lakewood's downtown. The 140-acre site will contain 1.1 million square feet of retail, restaurant, and entertainment space; 900,000 square feet of office and hotel space; and 1,300 residential units in an urban mix of town houses, lofts, live-work units, and condominium and rental apartments. The project also includes an arts center, urban park, skating rink, and three public parking structures. In awarding the redevelopment the 2006 award for best mixed use project, the Urban Land Institute noted that Belmar celebrates "the public realm over the private realm. At Belmar, streets are more important than any buildings on them, and parks and plazas are more important than the buildings that surround them." This suburban retrofit contributes to sustainability by replacing a large declining, auto-oriented private shopping mall with an urban, mixed use downtown served by public transit.

Chapter 6

Dynamic Financial Analysis

The feasibility of projects whose income and expenditures are spread over several years is assessed with *dynamic financial analysis.* For these projects, the timing of money inflows and outflows is a critical consideration. In chapters 3 and 4, we considered development alternatives whose feasibility can be assessed at one point in time, using the static techniques of cost-driven and market-driven analyses. This chapter explains dynamic financial analysis and describes its main technique—discounted cash flow analysis—including its terminology. We provide an illustrative example with calculations.

Discounted cash flow (DCF) analysis is the financial feasibility technique used to evaluate expenditures and returns from developing or investing in income-generating properties, including office, retail, industrial (warehouse and flex space), lodging, and multifamily residential development (primarily apartments). Mixed use projects also include for-sale residential units, which are often legally structured as condominiums. Although they do not generate income over time, for-sale properties are handled in discounted cash flow analysis by including revenues from sales in the time period when they occur.

In order to apply discounted cash flow analysis properly, it is important to understand basic finance concepts. Along with a description of the discounted cash flow analysis technique, this chapter defines the important financial terms, such as *compounding* and *discounting*, and gives an example of how to apply discounted cash flow analysis. The discussion is geared to designers, planners, and other readers whose familiarity with financial concepts and terminology is limited. This may have prevented them from attempting to apply discounted cash flow as an alternative analysis tool, thinking it too arcane or complicated for their purposes. We believe that, while the computations are complicated, the basic logic is straightforward and the learning is important. As Williamson (2013, 43) notes, "The road ahead may require designers to become even more knowledgeable than they already are about real estate financing and pro forma financial statements so as to find the most effective ways to argue for the market value and potential returns—both economic and ecological—of good design and durable, high quality materials and methods." The same could be said for city planners writing the rules for urban development.

Discounted Cash Flow Analysis Logic

Discounted cash flow analysis looks at the income and expenditures of a proposed development project over time. Whereas cost-driven and market-driven analyses are static techniques that examine project feasibility at one point in time, discounted cash flow analysis is a dynamic technique that accounts for the important influences of time on costs and returns over the life of a project. The discounted cash flow analysis template is used to keep track of all cash inflows and outflows over time. It is similar to the one used in chapter 5 to conduct revenue-expense analysis.[1]

Discounted cash flow analysis enables real estate developers and investors to compare cost to value, taking time into account. The technique is based on the *time value of money*—the reasonable idea that consumption now is preferred to consumption later. A borrower who wants to use money for development now is willing to pay interest to a lender as compensation for the lender's willingness to wait for repayment of the loan in the future.

In turn, lenders such as commercial banks pay interest to savers, who are the source of their funds. That interest is compounded. Compounding works this way: Interest is paid on the initial amount of savings in the first period. In the second period, interest is paid on the entire amount, which includes the interest that was initially paid. In the third period, the savings account balance includes two previous interest payments plus the original deposit. Interest is again paid on the entire amount, and so on. Thus, compounding results in an exponential increase in value moving from the present to the future. For example, a dollar saved today at an annual interest rate of 10 percent will be worth $1.10 in one year, $1.21 in two years, $1.33 in three years, and so on.

Discounting works just like compounding but moves in the opposite direction, from the future to the present. Cash to be received by the lender in the future is discounted to find its lower present value. For example, a dollar to be received from a project payout in 10 years discounted at 10 percent annually has a present value of $0.39.

Unlike interest rates, which are typically set by lenders on the basis of financial markets, discount rates are set by developers and investors using their own risk-return calculus. The rate at which future values are discounted to present values depends on time preferences. Those with long time horizons who are willing to defer consumption apply relatively low discount rates; others who highly value consumption in the near term have higher discount rates. Discount rates also increase as perceived risk increases.

Private investors estimate their *opportunity cost of capital* to arrive at an appropriate discount rate. The opportunity cost of capital depends on many factors but essentially reflects the expected

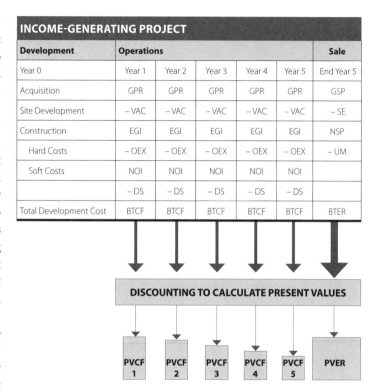

Figure 6-4. Return on Investment Structure

return on other investment opportunities, taking anticipated risk levels into account. Developers and investors use discount rates in the 8–15 percent range for speculative commercial development projects. Infill and redevelopment projects tend to be in the high range to reflect greater perceived risk.

Planners and designers do not need to know the formulas behind discounted cash flow analysis, but they should become familiar enough with its terms and logic to understand how spreadsheet results are generated. With this understanding, they can see how their decisions may affect the feasibility of proposed development projects. At this point, readers unfamiliar with the language of discounted cash flow analysis may want to look over the glossary of real estate development terms. They should then review the appendix to this chapter, including the discounted cash flow example and the discounted cash flow analysis computations. Figure 6-4 should help readers visualize how net present value (NPV) is calculated on a before-tax basis.

The length of the time periods used in dynamic models depends on the purpose of the analysis. For development projects, monthly time periods are used to analyze *solvency*, as they were for the revenue-expense analysis conducted in chapter 5. To assess the *financial returns* of either a development project or an investment, annual periods are usually employed in the discounted cash flow analysis model.

In the static cost-driven and market-driven analyses presented earlier, return on equity was cash-on-cash return (before-tax cash flow per dollar of invested equity at stabilized occupancy). To assess the project's attractiveness as an investment opportunity with dynamic analysis, investors use *net present value* (NPV) and *internal rate of return* (IRR). The present value of future cash flows is found using the developer's or investor's discount rate. Net present value is the difference between this computed present value and the initial investment, which occurs in the present time period. If the NPV is positive, the development or investment opportunity is attractive.

Internal rate of return is the discount rate at which the present value of the future cash flows from operations and from the prop-

erty sale exactly equals the initial investment and the NPV is zero. Before-tax IRR for investments that are all equity—that is, when no debt or "leverage" is involved—are attractive in the 6–12 percent range. When both debt and equity comprise the investment capital, the leveraged IRR range is higher.

If the developer wants to get a completely accurate estimate of returns, investments made over a period of more than one year should not be assumed to have occurred within one year. For instance, for a project that took three years to develop and was held for 10 years, the discounted cash flow analysis would have to account for all positive and negative cash flows during the 14-year period. In most instances, however, all investments are assumed to occur in one year (Year 0). The additional information needed for a development project is the capital budget, which lays out the cost of the proposed development. The capital budgets presented in chapter 7 include more-detailed versions of the development cost categories used in the cost-driven and market-driven analyses described in chapter 3.

Application of Discounted Cash Flow Analysis

Developers focus primarily on the market opportunities and the development costs associated with income-generating projects they are considering. Planners are usually not concerned with project costs. Designers may be aware of rents, sales prices, or development costs, but usually at a general level. The financial analysis presented in the appendix to this chapter should help designers and planners understand how developers compare cost to value for more complex income-generating properties. The analysis is not difficult to apply yet certainly represents a vast improvement over the ballpark figures often used.

The analysis of mixed use projects requires that each income-generating property type and for-sale residential property be analyzed *separately*. Potential investors need property-specific information because they are comparing the mixed use project to other opportunities, which are typically single-use projects, or to market averages, which are computed for each property type. Therefore, NPV and IRR for each income-generating property in the mixed use project need to be calculated.

The recommended way to conduct comprehensive financial feasibility analysis for income-generating properties involves five stages: 1) simple capitalization of stabilized NOI, 2) discounted cash flow analysis of annual cash flows for the hold period, 3) combined analysis of cash flows for the development and operating period, 4) monthly cash flows during the development period, and 5) discounted cash flow analysis for project investors (Peiser and Hamilton 2012, 168–91). Although developers may want to conduct all of these related stages of analysis, designers and planners need less complicated templates to follow. In chapter 7, we provide an analytical framework at an appropriate level of detail. To account for cost, a capital budget for the entire project and for each income-generating property type is needed; to estimate value, discounted cash flow analysis, which accounts for all revenues and expenses over time, is required.

Streamlining the Discounted Cash Flow Analysis

The discounted cash flow analysis presented for the infill redevelopment project in chapter 7 will be simplified in four ways: First, we will not consider the impact of income taxation on returns. Clearly, investors are interested in after-tax IRR, which accounts for federal and state income tax liability. They also want to know how much the sale of the property will generate after taxes are paid. However, the tax situation for each individual investor is likely to be different. Investors can take the before-tax analysis and conduct their own analysis to estimate after-tax returns.

Separate discounted cash flow analysis would usually be employed to analyze the for-sale units. The costs of horizontal development to build these units would be treated in each period as cash outflows. Net proceeds from sales (sales price less selling expenses) minus any unpaid construction loan balance would be cash inflows. These figures would be used to calculate the before-tax IRR for the for-sale units.

The second simplification will be to assume that the developer in this case will build and operate the nonresidential uses only. After horizontal development is completed, the developer will sell sites for the other uses. In the infill case, then, separate analysis of for-sale property is not necessary.

The third simplification pertains to the time dimension. Typically, developers examine monthly and quarterly cash flows, and they usually hold income-generating properties for 10 years or more. In this analysis, we will divide the time dimension into annual periods, and we will assume that the hold period is only seven years, after which the property is sold. Therefore, after returns from each income-generating property are calculated separately for the seven-year hold period, the figures for the for-sale residential properties and the commercial properties will be incorporated into one summary discounted cash flow analysis to gauge the before-tax IRR for the entire project.

In the redevelopment project from which the infill case is drawn, the developer proposed a mix of single-use and multiuse buildings. The financial model can easily accommodate mixed use projects with both types of buildings. The fourth and final simplification of the financial model will be to assume that only single-use buildings will be constructed.

Chapter 7 presents an example of the use of discounted cash flow analysis to assess the financial feasibility of a mixed use infill redevelopment project drawn from a real-world case. This grounded application should be helpful for readers who may still have questions about the logic and utility of discounted cash flow analysis. It also demonstrates how the technique can be useful in making a comparison between the financial implications of project revisions resulting from community reactions and the financial returns reflected in the original project application. In that case, the initial project proposal was substantially changed as the result of working for several years with the project neighbors to improve its acceptability to the community. Changes in the design led to corresponding changes in development returns, as shown in the discounted cash flow analysis, whose bottom lines revealed that a further round of design changes would be needed to make the project feasible.

Summary: Dynamic Financial Analysis

The feasibility of development projects whose income and expenditures are spread over several years is assessed with dynamic financial analysis. For these projects, the timing of money inflows and outflows is a critical consideration. Discounted cash flow analysis is the financial feasibility technique used to evaluate expenditures and returns from developing or investing in income-generating properties.

Discount rates—the rates at which future values are discounted to present values—depend on time preferences. Those with long time horizons who are willing to defer consumption apply lower discount rates; others who highly value consumption in the near term have higher discount rates. Discount rates also increase as perceived risk increases.

This chapter presents the logic of discounted cash flow analysis and describes how it can be used to examine development projects. It also explains how we simplify and streamline the analysis provided in chapter 7. The discounted cash flow analysis example in the appendix should help the reader understand the logic and use of this dynamic analysis technique.

Appendix to Chapter 6
Discounted Cash Flow Analysis Example

The calculations described in this example generate the estimates needed to analyze returns using discounted cash flow analysis. The items included are essentially the same as those in the cost-driven and market-driven analyses presented in chapter 3. If the project is funded entirely with equity, the owner or investors receive NOI. More typically, the project is leveraged by obtaining a mortgage loan, and the lender is paid debt service (DS), which is determined by the amount, interest rate, and amortization period of the loan. The amortization of this loan, which assumes annual payments, is shown in table 6-3.

In this example, we assume that the lender provides 70 percent of the financing ($997,500), and the equity investors provide the remaining 30 percent of the $1,425,000 development cost or investment. Because the project is leveraged, the equity portion of the investment is compared to the present value of net cash inflows to calculate returns. If the project or investment was financed entirely with equity, the total cost of the project or investment would be used to calculate returns.

Before-tax cash flow (BTCF) is forecast for the hold period of five years. Net operating income for the sixth year is included to calculate the gross sales price (GSP). An 11 percent going-out capitalization rate appropriate for this project is used to find the gross sales price using the basic equation for estimating the value of an asset that generates future income: Value = NOI ÷ capitalization rate. The going-in capitalization rate of 10.27 percent equals stabilized NOI ($146,400 in Year 1) divided by the total investment of $1.425 million. The going-out rate is 73 basis points higher than the going-in rate. (See glossary of real estate development terms for definitions.)

By convention, going-out capitalization rates are usually 50–200 basis points higher than going-in rates. This convention draws on the following logic: We should reflect the fact that the future is uncertain by forecasting the future value of assets conservatively. Higher capitalization rates achieve this by lowering value. Second, assets depreciate and become obsolete over time. Buildings that are seven years old should be less valuable than newer ones. The higher going-out capital-ization rate reduces value notwithstanding the fact that NOI usually increases over time.

The developer or investor keeps track of income tax liability in the accounts called the IRS Books. The IRS treats interest paid (INT) and depreciation expenses (DEP) as legitimate deductions from NOI. The tax payment (TAX) is brought into the Investor's Books to enable the calculation of after-tax cash flow (ATCF).

The cash flow from sale occurs at the end of the fifth year. The gross sales price less selling expenses (SE) gives the net sales price (NSP). Before-tax equity reversion (BTER), or residual, from the sale of the project is found by deducting the amount needed to pay off the balance due on the loan (UM) from the net sales price. The unpaid balance is the amount shown in bold in the amortization table at the end of the fifth year.

Accumulated depreciation is taxed at sale because it is a noncash expense deducted from income during the hold period that reduces tax liability at the marginal tax rate (MTR). Some of this tax benefit enjoyed over the hold period is "recaptured" at sale. Notice that the 25 percent recapture tax rate (RCR) is higher than the capital gains rate (CGR) of 15 percent but lower than the marginal tax rate of 33 percent. Total taxes due are deducted from the before-tax equity reversion to get after-tax equity reversion (ATER).

To find NPV, we assume that the investors use a discount rate of 15 percent to reflect their opportunity cost of capital. At this rate, NPV is positive, indicating an attractive investment opportunity. The NPV function in Excel calculates the present value of five years of positive cash flows and compares that sum to the initial $427,500 investment (negative cash flow) at the specified discount rate. The difference between total present value and initial investment is NPV. Positive NPV means that the IRR will be greater than 15 percent. Remember that IRR is the rate at which NPV equals 0. In this example, the before-tax IRR is 21.1 percent, and the after-tax IRR is 16.8 percent.

Returns are usually partitioned to distinguish cash flows generated during the hold period from the residual cash flow from the sale of the project. The former are deemed less risky than the latter for two reasons. First, annual cash flows are received sooner than the residual cash flow. Second, the residual depends on one sale event rather than ongoing management of the project. For projects held for the same period of time, the higher the residual contribution to returns, the riskier is the project. Partitioning before-tax returns in this case indicates that 42 percent comes from operations, and the remaining 58 percent comes from the sale of the project.

This illustrative case of a development or investment opportunity appears to be sufficiently profitable to attract the equity needed to finance the project. The internal rates of return are high enough to make the time and cost of development and subsequent ownership worth the risks involved.

TABLE 6-1. CASH FLOWS FROM OPERATIONS: EXAMPLE

A. PROPERTY CASH FLOWS

	Year 1	Year 2	Year 3	Year 4	Year 5	Year 6
Gross Potential Revenue	$259,200	$272,160	$285,768	$300,056	$315,059	$330,812
– Vacancy	$10,800	$11,340	$11,907	$12,502	$13,127	$13,784
= Effective Gross Income	$248,400	$260,820	$273,861	$287,554	$301,932	$317,028
– Operating Expenses	$102,000	$107,100	$112,455	$118,078	$123,982	$130,181
= Net Operating Income (NOI)	$146,400	$153,720	$161,406	$169,476	$177,950	$186,848

B. FINANCING CASH FLOWS

	Year 1	Year 2	Year 3	Year 4	Year 5	Year 6
Net Operating Income (NOI)	$146,400	$153,720	$161,406	$169,476	$177,950	
– Debt Service	$97,093	$97,093	$97,093	$97,093	$97,093	
= Before-tax Cash Flow	$49,307	$56,627	$64,313	$72,383	$80,857	

C. TAX CASH FLOWS

1. IRS Books

	Year 1	Year 2	Year 3	Year 4	Year 5	Year 6
Net Operating Income (NOI)	$146,400	$153,720	$161,406	$169,476	$177,950	
– Interest Paid	$89,775	$89,116	$88,398	$87,616	$86,763	
– Depreciation	$38,691	$38,691	$38,691	$38,691	$38,691	
= Taxable Income	$17,934	$25,913	$34,317	$43,169	$52,496	
× Marginal Tax Rate	33%	33%	33%	33%	33%	
= Tax	$5,918	$8,551	$11,324	$14,246	$17,324	

2. Investor's Books

	Year 1	Year 2	Year 3	Year 4	Year 5	Year 6
Net Operating Income (NOI)	$146,400	$153,720	$161,406	$169,476	$177,950	
– Debt Service	$97,093	$97,093	$97,093	$97,093	$97,093	
= Before-Tax Cash Flow	$49,307	$56,627	$64,313	$72,383	$80,857	
– Tax	$5,918	$8,551	$11,324	$14,246	$17,324	
= After-Tax Cash Flow	$43,389	$48,076	$52,989	$58,137	$63,533	

TABLE 6-2. CASH FLOWS FROM DISPOSITION: EXAMPLE

A. PROPERTY CASH FLOWS

Gross Sales Price	$1,698,618		
– Selling Expenses	$101,917		
= Net Sales Price	$1,596,701		

B. FINANCING CASH FLOWS

Net Sales Price	$1,596,701		
– Unpaid Mortgage Balance	$953,704		
= Before-Tax Equity Reversion	$642,997		

C. TAX CASH FLOWS

1. IRS Books

Tax on Gain		Tax on Recapture	
Net Sales Price	$1,596,701	Accumulated Depreciation	$193,455
– Original Development Cost or Investment	$1,425,000	× Recapture Tax Rate	25%
= Gain	$171,701	Recapture Tax	$48,364
× Capital Gains Rate	15%		
Capital Gains Tax	$25,755		
Total Tax	$74,119		

2. Equity Investor's Books

Before-Tax Equity Reversion	$642,997		
– Total Tax	$74,119		
= After-Tax Equity Reversion	$568,878		

RESULTS

Before-tax IRR = 21.07 percent, and NPV = $88,478 with 15 percent discount rate

After-tax IRR = 16.82 percent, and NPV – $25,200 with 15% discount rate

Portion of before-tax returns from operations: 42 percent

Portion of before-tax returns from residual: 58 percent

TABLE 6-3. AMORTIZATION TABLE FOR LOAN: EXAMPLE

Original Loan Balance	$997,500
Loan Rate	9%
Loan Term	30 years

YEAR	STARTING BALANCE	PAYMENT	INTEREST	PRINCIPAL	ENDING BALANCE
1	$997,500	$97,093	$89,775	$7,318	$990,182
2	$990,182	$97,093	$89,116	$7,977	$982,205
3	$982,205	$97,093	$88,398	$8,695	$973,511
4	$973,511	$97,093	$87,616	$9,477	$964,034
5	$964,034	$97,093	$86,763	$10,330	**$953,704**
6	$953,704	$97,093	$85,833	$11,260	$942,444
7	$942,444	$97,093	$84,820	$12,273	$930,171
8	$930,171	$97,093	$83,715	$13,378	$916,794
9	$916,794	$97,093	$82,511	$14,582	$902,212
10	$902,212	$97,093	$81,199	$15,894	$886,318
11	$886,318	$97,093	$79,769	$17,324	$868,994
12	$868,994	$97,093	$78,209	$18,884	$850,110
13	$850,110	$97,093	$76,510	$20,583	$829,527
14	$829,527	$97,093	$74,657	$22,436	$807,091
15	$807,091	$97,093	$72,638	$24,455	$782,637
16	$782,637	$97,093	$70,437	$26,656	$755,981
17	$755,981	$97,093	$68,038	$29,055	$726,926
18	$726,926	$97,093	$65,423	$31,670	$695,256
19	$695,256	$97,093	$62,573	$34,520	$660,736
20	$660,736	$97,093	$59,466	$37,627	$623,110
21	$623,110	$97,093	$56,080	$41,013	$582,097
22	$582,097	$97,093	$52,389	$44,704	$537,392
23	$537,392	$97,093	$48,365	$48,728	$488,665
24	$488,665	$97,093	$43,980	$53,113	$435,551
25	$435,551	$97,093	$39,200	$57,893	$377,658
26	$377,658	$97,093	$33,989	$63,104	$314,554

TABLE 6-3. AMORTIZATION TABLE FOR LOAN: EXAMPLE

Original Loan Balance	$997,500
Loan Rate	9%
Loan Term	30 years

YEAR	STARTING BALANCE	PAYMENT	INTEREST	PRINCIPAL	ENDING BALANCE
27	$314,554	$97,093	$28,310	$68,783	$245,771
28	$245,771	$97,093	$22,119	$74,974	$170,797
29	$170,797	$97,093	$15,372	$81,721	$89,076
30	$89,076	$97,093	$8,017	$89,076	$0

(Initial case by David J. Hartzell, Stephen D. Bell and Leonard W. Wood Distinguished Professor in Real Estate, Kenan-Flagler Business School, University of North Carolina at Chapel Hill, with revisions by the authors.)

Santana Row, San Jose, California

DEVELOPER: Federal Realty Investment Trust

ARCHITECTS: SB Architects, BAR Architects, Steinberg Architects, STUDIOS

LANDSCAPE ARCHITECTS: SWA Group, April Philips Design Works

WEBSITE: www.santanarow.com/more/

Santana Row is a $450 million, 1.5 million-square-foot mixed use "village within a city" in San Jose, California. The project replaced a 43-acre strip shopping center with a new landscaped urban "main street" center. Opening in 2002 just 80 days after a major fire that caused $130 million in damage, the center has proven to be enormously successful. As of 2012, its pedestrian-friendly sidewalks drew some 30,000 visitors a day for shopping and dining in its 70 shops and 20 restaurants. The four blocks of the 1,500-foot-long main street, lined with arcaded shops and three- to five-story buildings, create a lively, popular "outoor room." Its mix of uses includes 834 residential units, office space for 350 employees, a movie theater, two parks, and a five-star hotel. Its 2008 LEED Gold six-story office tower, 300 Santana Row, includes 65,000 square feet of Class A space over a two-story retail base, as well as a stand-alone parking structure. Santana Row was named 2010 Project of the Decade by the Silicon Valley Business Journal for its transformational and economic impact on the Silicon Valley area.

From top to bottom: Figure 7-1. Hotel Valencia, Santana Row (Courtesy of Charles C. Bohl.); Figure 7-2. Santana Row Streetscape (Courtesy of Charles C. Bohl.); Figure 7-3. Site Plan of Santana Row, San Jose, California (Courtesy of Federal Realty Investment Trust.)

Chapter 7
Infill Redevelopment Alternatives

Infill development and redevelopment are critical components of urban growth. As cities build out their cores and urban growth expands beyond the inner ring suburbs, opportunities arise to intensify development in their centers. More intense central city land use contributes to reduced future sprawl, makes more efficient use of existing infrastructure, and improves overall accessibility. Usually such infill development or redevelopment replaces existing lower-density or obsolete structures with higher-density, mixed use projects (Dunham-Jones and Williamson 2011).

Mixed use infill development projects are more complex and challenging than single-use and greenfield projects. The design challenge is to create a workable combination of uses that achieves coherence and synergies within the project and is compatible with and connected to the existing context of surrounding neighborhoods and land uses. The development challenge is to create a feasible financial calculus that accounts for investment capital, project costs, and multiple income streams over the life of the project. The planning challenge is to envision, plan, and operate a regulatory process that guides development toward sustainable outcomes. This involves responding to market forces for core-area redevelopment, concerns about neighborhood compatibility and development impacts, and the need for consistency with plans at the small-area, city, and regional scales.

This chapter describes and analyzes a case of mixed use infill redevelopment to show how dynamic financial analysis, presented in chapter 6, can be used to assess planning and design alternatives. In doing so, we also provide another example of the connections among the roles of designers, developers, and planners. Because of their longer time horizon and more complex financial arrangements, mixed use infill projects are best understood with the use of dynamic financial analysis, which captures the projected flow of transactions that occur from the start of a project to its conclusion. We present the analysis for an infill redevelopment project and then compare its financial feasibility to that of a revised version of the project. After the case and the analysis are presented, we briefly consider ways to improve infill redevelopment projects.

Initial Infill Redevelopment Proposal

This case concerns the redevelopment of a 70-acre post–World War II apartment and retail complex in Chapel Hill, North Carolina, into a contemporary mixed use infill project.[1] Built as a housing opportunity for returning veterans seeking education at the University of North Carolina, which is only 1 mile to the west of the site, the original complex was designed as low-density, suburban-style rental housing with an adjacent neighborhood shopping center. It contains 440 units of rental housing, ranging in size from 680 to 1,275 square feet, and 26,032 square feet of commercial development in a small neighborhood center originally anchored by a grocery store, and other nonresidential uses.

TABLE 7-1. PROPOSED USES: BASE CASE

Use Types	Numbers
Single-Family Residential	27 units
Multifamily Residential	745 units
Apartments	250 units
For-sale	495 units
Hotel	140 rooms
Retail	234,500 SF
Grocery	55,000 SF
Cinema	700 seats
Restaurants and Shops	144,500 SF
Office	262,000 SF
Parking Total	2,572 spaces
Decked	1,930 spaces
Surface	642 spaces

Source: Glen Lennox Concept Plan Proposal, April 2008. Grubb Properties.

As shown in figure 7-4, the site is distinguished by its dense apartment layout, compared with the adjacent lower-density single-family neighborhoods. It is bounded by major arterial roads: U.S. 15-501 on the west and N.C. 54 on the south. (Note that north is to the right side in the figure.) On the east and north sides, it is adjacent to mature, owner-occupied single-family residential neighborhoods. Its internal road circulation pattern consists of suburban-style curvilinear roads. The site is heavily wooded. The area along N.C. 54 has changed significantly since the project was originally developed. Recent major developments include a mixed use retail, office, hotel, and residential condominium project laterally across N.C. 54 and a large in-town new town a half mile further east (both of these newer developments are outside the area shown on the figure).

The property owner—who leads a successful commercial real estate development company based in Charlotte, North Carolina—wanted to explore alternative development schemes to convert the property into a mixed use high-density urban project. In 2008, he requested rezoning of the property from R-3 and CC (Community Commercial) to MU-V-Arterial (Mixed Use). The original redevelopment concept plan, proposed in 2008, contemplated removing most of the existing structures in order to carry out development of new office, retail, and residential uses, with parking on streets, in decks, and on surface lots. This plan called for 1,582,000 square feet of total floor area with 772 dwelling units, at a gross density of 11 units per acre. The floor area ratio ranged from 1.0 for retail to 4.0 for apartments and a hotel. For-sale residential and office floor area ratios were about 2.5. The floor area mix was 62 percent residential and 36 percent office, retail, or hotel, with 80,000 square feet of recreation space. The proposed uses complied with the MU-V-Arterial zoning, except for the parking, which was over by 726 spaces. Included in the count were 244 on-street parking spaces. (See table 7-1.)

In his statement of compliance with the town's development guidelines, the developer stated that his proposal would:

- further the goal of creating a compact urban form of development, without requiring expansion of existing public facilities or infrastructure;
- maintain the town's urban services area by providing housing, office, and commercial opportunities at this close-in, well-served location;
- further the goal of creating a walkable community with less reliance on the automobile by developing this site with new mixed uses within walking distance of established areas;
- work toward a balanced transportation system through adding uses to a site on existing bus routes and adjacent to the N.C. 54 pedestrian and bike greenway;
- encourage desirable forms of nonresidential development by placing destination activities on established bus, bike, and pedestrian routes;
- prevent increases in stormwater drainage quantity and quality through on-site detention, retention, and reuse facilities; and

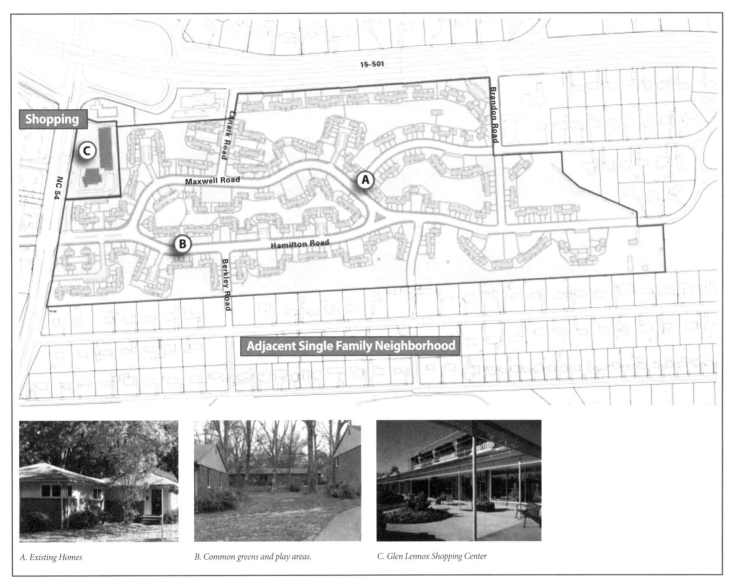

A. Existing Homes

B. Common greens and play areas.

C. Glen Lennox Shopping Center

Figure 7-4. Existing Conditions. (Adapted from Urban Design Associates, 2012. Courtesy of Grubb Properties and Urban Design Associates.)

- help create affordable housing opportunities through increased diversity of both rental and for-sale residential units.

The proposed concept plan, which showed the design at build-out, placed three large parking decks in the center of the site, faced with multifamily residential, retail, and mixed use buildings. Office buildings ranging in height from two to five stories were clustered around the main entrance from N.C. 54, adjoined by one-story retail buildings. One-story retail buildings and a hotel that was five to seven stories high faced U.S. 15-501 on the west side. Multifamily residential lined the east edge of the site, adjacent to the existing single-family residential neighborhood. New single-family lots were located on the northeast corner. A potential civic-use building was adjacent to the existing church on the northwest corner. (See figure 7-5.)

The project was proposed to be developed in three phases. First, the central core uses and the buildings facing U.S. 15-501 on the west were to be built. Next to be built were the residential uses adjacent to the existing neighborhood on the east, and the hotel on the west. Finally, the commercial and office uses facing N.C. 54 on the south were to be built.

The actual length of time required for these phases would be determined by local politics and future market conditions. It could take several years to receive public approvals, given the complexity of the project, and two to three more years to complete a phase of construction. Thus, the first phase could be completed five years in the future and the second phase two to three years later. The final phase may not begin until the ninth or 10th year. The analysis of financial returns would begin when significant expenditures were incurred and end 20 or 25 years in the future, depending on the length of the hold period.

Financial Analysis of Initial Infill Redevelopment Proposal

Large-scale redevelopment projects often involve a master developer, who gets the project approved, and then one or more sub-developers, who develop uses or areas within the project. At one extreme, the master developer develops all proposed uses except the one for which he or she lacks expertise or experience. At the other extreme, the master developer sells the land to specialized developers, who implement the plan for each use or specific site. In this situation, the master developer becomes a land developer, similarly to the one examined in chapter 5. The discounted cash flow analysis compares land development costs to land sales occurring over time. The properties developed by others would enter the discounted cash flow analysis of income-generating uses as property sales in the year they were executed, along with the associated costs.[2]

We assume that the master developer will focus on the retail and office properties only and sell parcels to others to develop the residential uses—namely, the hotel, apartments, town houses, higher-density residential, and single-family detached housing. One or more development companies will be selected to build the apartments and multifamily for-sale units, the mix of which will be determined by market conditions. Local home builders will be selected to assume responsibility for the single-family units. A hotel chain will be recruited to build the hotel. Most major hotel chains have developers that build their facilities on a regional basis.

To simplify the financial analysis, we have reduced the original phasing from three phases to two, drastically compressing the development timeline. We assume that all land development costs are incurred and all of the retail and office construction is completed in Year 0. Development of the parking decks is also completed in Year 0. Stabilized occupancy for retail and office uses is achieved at the beginning of Year 1, which is equivalent to assuming that the commercial development is fully preleased. These income-generating properties are held for seven years and then sold.

In the second phase, the multifamily parcels, the hotel site, and the single-family parcels are sold. Revenues from these sales are received in years 2, 3, and 4, respectively.

While we have simplified the framework by reducing the number of time periods, in order to make the computations less exten-

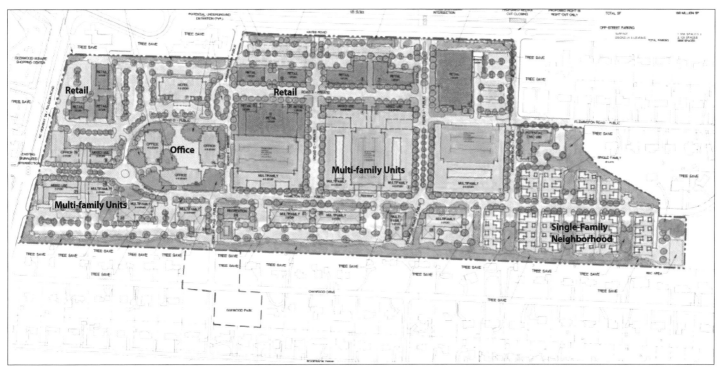

Figure 7-5. Proposed Concept Plan Design (Adapted from the Concept Plan. Grubb Properties, GGA Architects, and Ballentine Engineers. 2008. Used by permission.)

sive, the framework has not been simplified conceptually. Within this dynamic framework, the financial analysis compares cost to value. Project costs are accounted for in the capital budget, which includes the cost of land, demolition, infrastructure and other site development, parking structures and lots, hard costs, associated soft costs, and financing costs. Construction and development fees and related contingencies are included in the soft costs.

The capital budget represents the uses of funds for this development project. The sources of funds are debt and equity. Permanent mortgage loans for the office development and retail development are based on typical underwriting criteria. Investors usually generate the equity to cover the remaining financing needed. In this case, the land,

which is owned by the developer, provides the equity needed to complete the financing.

We assume no public subsidies. In practice, many large-scale mixed use redevelopment projects are subsidized by the public. The Low-Income Housing Tax Credit, Historic Preservation Tax Incentives, and New Markets Tax Credit are three federal programs that are used to subsidize development. States have comparable programs, as well as loans and grants for such projects. Local governments also provide their own financial subsidies.

Capital budgets that specify development cost for the retail and office uses enable separate analyses of these income-generating properties. The estimations involve accounting for hard costs for office and retail development, plus a portion of site development, parking, soft costs, and financing costs. The difference between these development costs and the total development cost is the cost of horizontal development associated with the sites to be sold to other developers and home builders. Therefore, the capital budget has sub-budgets for these two commercial uses. The development costs are shown in table 7-2.

The analysis begins with the original 70-acre developed site valued at $40.8 million. The total cost for horizontal development without associated soft costs is estimated to be $80.7 million. Hard costs amount to only $67.3 million, because only about 30 percent of the square footage—the retail and office properties—will be built by the developer. Soft costs and financing costs bring the total cost of the development to $167.1 million.

The table also shows the assignment of costs associated with retail and office development, $48.3 million and $50.3 million, respectively. The permanent loan for retail development is underwritten at an 80 percent loan-to-value ratio and a 1.15 debt-service coverage ratio. The result is a loan of $40.7 million. Underwriting for the office development is more conservative, with a 75 percent loan-to-value ratio and a 1.25 debt-service coverage ratio. The resulting loan is $38.4 million. The equity line shows the remaining amounts needed to cover the development costs for retail and office development given their respective permanent loan amounts.

The second panel of table 7-2 presents the allocation of costs and equity. After accounting for the income-generating properties, $68.5 million is the cost of horizontal development for the residential and hotel sites. From total equity, $22.4 million remains to be associated with the horizontal development. The difference between these two numbers is the estimated construction loan balance to be repaid from site sales, $46.1 million.[3]

The figures in table 7-2 were adapted from information that the developer provided. Designers and planners can gather comparable information in several ways. Local general contractors, architecture and engineering firms, and other professional engineers can provide reliable information on current development costs. As mentioned in chapter 3, RSMeans produces very useful construction-cost information on a national basis, as do several other firms. Loan officers with financial institutions that provide construction and permanent loans can help estimate financing amounts and costs. After information has been gathered from these sources, we recommend meeting with several active local developers to get their input on the overall and unit cost statistics that were gathered. With this corroboration, development cost estimates should be reliable. Annual reviews should be sufficient to keep the numbers current.

The anticipated revenues and operating expenses for the retail and office development at stabilized occupancy are presented in table 7-3. The categories are the same as those presented in the appendix to chapter 6. The discounted cash flow analysis compares the present value of cash flows from operations and from the sale of the property to the equity needed to develop the retail or office property. This comparison is used to generate the NPV and IRR before income taxes.

Table 7-3 shows all the important assumptions used to conduct the analysis. The retail structures are highly efficient in that the area on which rent is charged is 90 percent of total area built (GBA). Office buildings are 85 percent efficient on average. The rent for retail is lower than office rent, as is the vacancy allowance. The lower retail rent partly reflects the fact that some operating expenses will be paid by tenants. Operating expenses are therefore higher for office than for retail.[4] Tax and growth rates are the same for both retail and office. The total cost to develop each use in table 7-2 is shown next.

It is estimated that when the properties are sold, selling expenses will be 6 percent. The underwriting assumptions noted above are shown for the retail and office loans. Both are charged interest at 5.1 percent, amortized over 30 years. The calculated debt-service coverage ratios for retail and office over seven years of operation meet or exceed their required ratios.

The remaining items are the capitalization rates. As explained in the appendix to chapter 6, terminal (going-out) capitalization rates are based on initial (going-in) capitalization rates. The going-out capi-

TABLE 7-2. INFILL REDEVELOPMENT PROJECT CAPITAL BUDGET

	Amount	$ per SF	Cost	Retail Cost	Office Cost
LAND DEVELOPMENT					
Land	3, 049,200 SF	$13.71	$41,804,532		
Demolition		$0.50	$1,524,600		
Site Work		$2.00	$6,098,400		
Off-Site Infrastructure		$0.50	$1,524,600		
Contingency					
Subtotal Site Development			$9,147,600		
Total Land Development			**$50,952,132**	$7,533,386	$8,448,722
PARKING		**$ per space**			
Structured	1,930 spaces	$15,000	$28,950,000		
Surface	642 spaces	$1,200	$770,400		
Total Parking			**$29,720,400**	$4,404,563	$4,927,642
HARD COSTS					
Construction	GBA	**$ per SF**			
Retail	234,500 SF	$95.00	$22,277,500	$22,277,500	
Office	262,000 SF	$92.00	$24,104,000		$24,104,000
Tenant Improvements					
Retail	234,500 SF	$35.00	$8,207,500	$8,207,500	
Office	262,000 SF	$25.00	$6,550,000		$6,550,000
Subtotal Hard Costs			$61,139,000		
Contingency		at 10%	$6,113,900	$3,056,950	$3,056,950
Total Hard Costs			**$67,252,900**	$33,541,950	$33,710,950
SOFT COSTS		**% Hard Costs**			
Fees and Other Soft Costs		18%	$12,105,522		
Total Soft Costs			**$12,105,522**	$1,794,038	$2,007,096
TOTAL DEVELOPMENT COSTS (Before Financing)			**$160,030,954**		
FINANCING					
Construction Loan Amount (at 75% Loan to Cost)			$125,250,000		
Construction Loan Interest			$5,386,628		
Loan Fees			$1,670,000		
Construction Interest and Fee			$7,056,628		

Table 7–2 continues on the next page.

TABLE 7-2. INFILL REDEVELOPMENT PROJECT CAPITAL BUDGET

	Amount	$ per SF	Cost	Retail Cost	Office Cost
Total Financing Costs			**$7,056,628**	$1,045,792	$1,169,989
Total Development Costs (with Financing Costs)			**$167,087,582**	$48,339,730	$50,264,399
PERMANENT LOAN				$40,740,467	$38,438,020
EQUITY				$7,599,263	$11,826,379
TOTAL DEVELOPMENT COSTS			$167,087,582		
Retail Development Costs			$48,339,730		
Office Development Costs			$50,264,399		
Subtotal			$98,604,129		
Remaining Development Costs			$68,483,453		
Multifamily Residential			$63,085,236		
Hotel			$2,104,217		
Single-Family Residential			$3,294,000		
TOTAL EQUITY			$41,804,532		
Retail Equity			$7,599,263		
Office Equity			$11,826,379		
Subtotal			$19,425,642		
Remaining Equity			$22,378,890		
Remaining Construction Loan Balance			$46,104,563		

talization rates used here are 1 percent (or 100 basis points) higher than the going-in rates. The going-in rates are 6 percent for retail and 7.5 percent for office. The capitalization rates mean that investors expect to make $6.00 or $7.50 for investing $100 in retail or office property, respectively. This difference indicates that the market considers office development riskier than retail development, because investors need to earn $1.50 more on a $100 office investment than on a $100 retail investment. Office rent is higher than retail rent, and vacancies are substantially higher. These market conditions are consistent with the more conservative underwriting applied to office property.

The going-in capitalization rates have another important purpose. We use them to find the initial value of stabilized property. For retail, the 6 percent capitalization rate is divided into NOI for Year

1, when stabilized occupancy is expected. The result is $50,925,583. The permanent loan for retail is 80 percent of this value. Dividing Year 1 NOI for office by 7.5 percent generates a value of $51,250,693. The permanent loan for office is 75 percent of this value. These loan amounts are shown above in table 7-2.

The results for retail and office development shown in table 7-3 directly apply these assumptions to find NOI for Year 1. The figures for the next seven years apply the 2 percent growth rate to the first-year figures. Although the hold period is seven years, we calculate NOI in Year 8. This value divided by the appropriate going-out capitalization rate gives the sales price at the end of Year 7.

To estimate before-tax cash flows and equity reversion requires the use of an amortization table. The 30-year, 5.1 percent loan requires monthly debt-service payments of about $221,000 for retail and about $209,000 for office. The annual amounts are shown in the line below NOI in table 7-3. Remember that debt service is constant over the term of the loan. This is the main reason why before-tax cash flow increases over time. The other amount taken from the amortization table is the unpaid balance of the loan. The amounts shown for retail and office reflect the balance after 84 payments (seven years).

The cash flows and equity reversion are compared to invested equity to examine investment performance. We assume that $7.6 million is invested in retail development. The result is 12.1 percent IRR before taxes. When these cash flows are compared using a 10 percent discount rate, NPV is positive and over $800,000. Return

on cost is also shown, and it indicates that the developer earns $6.32 for every $100 of total development cost.

The identical calculations for office development show superior performance. The before-tax IRR is 15.3 percent, and NPV exceeds $3 million. Return on cost is also higher, at 7.65 percent. Note that $11.8 million in equity is needed for office given the permanent loan amount.

Now that results are shown separately for the income-generating properties, we can present the final spreadsheet, which includes the remaining invested equity and net revenues from parcel and site sales after paying off the construction loan. As noted, the master developer functions as a land developer com-

TABLE 7-3. INFILL REDEVELOPMENT PROJECT INVESTMENT ANAYLSIS FOR INCOME-GENERATING USES

ASSUMPTIONS

Rentable Building Area (RBA)—Retail	210,291 SF
RBA—Office	222,700 SF
Average Retail Rent per SF	$21.00
Office Rent per SF	$27.00
Vacancy Allowance—Retail	7.0%
Vacancy Allowance—Office	12.0%
Operating Expenses per SF—Retail	$3.50
Operating Expenses per SF—Office	$5.00
Real Estate Taxes per SF	$1.50
Annual Rent Growth	2.0%
Annual Expense Growth	2.0%
Development Cost—Retail	$48.3 million
Development Cost—Office	$50.3 million
Selling Expenses	6.0%
Going-Out Capitalization Rate—Retail	7.00%
Going-Out Capitalization Rate—Office	8.50%
Loan-to-Value Ratio—Retail	80%
Loan-to-Value Ratio—Office	75%
Permanent Loan: Interest Rate	5.1%
Permanent Loan: Term	30 years
Debt-Service Coverage Ratio—Retail	1.15
Debt-Service Coverage Ratio—Office	1.25

Table 7–3 continues on the next page.

TABLE 7-3. INFILL REDEVELOPMENT PROJECT INVESTMENT ANAYLSIS FOR INCOME-GENERATING USES

RETAIL DEVELOPMENT	YEARS								
	0	1	2	3	4	5	6	7	8
Gross Potential Revenue		$4,416,121	$4,504,443	$4,594,532	$4,686,423	$4,780,151	$4,875,754	$4,973,269	$5,072,735
– Vacancy Allowance		$309,128	$315,311	$321,617	$328,050	$334,611	$341,303	$348,129	$355,091
Effective Gross Income		$4,106,992	$4,189,132	$4,272,915	$4,358,373	$4,445,541	$4,534,451	$4,625,140	$4,717,643
– Operating Expenses		$736,020	$750,741	$765,755	$781,070	$796,692	$812,626	$828,878	$845,456
Real Estate Taxes		$315,437	$321,746	$328,181	$334,744	$341,439	$348,268	$355,234	$362,338
Net Operating Income (NOI)		$3,055,535	$3,116,646	$3,178,979	$3,242,558	$3,307,409	$3,373,558	$3,441,029	$3,509,849
– Debt Service		$2,654,403	$2,654,403	$2,654,403	$2,654,403	$2,654,403	$2,654,403	$2,654,403	
Before-Tax Cash Flow (BTCF)		$401,132	$462,243	$524,576	$588,155	$653,006	$719,155	$786,626	
Debt-Service Coverage Ratio—Retail		1.15	1.17	1.20	1.22	1.25	1.27	1.30	
Gross Sales Price								$50,140,704	
– Selling Expenses								$3,008,442	
Net Sales Price								$47,132,261	
– Unpaid Mortgage Balance								$35,901,724	
Before-Tax Equity Reversion (BTER)								$11,230, 537	
INVESTMENT PERFORMANCE									
Equity	-$7,599,263								
BTCF		$401,132	$462,243	$524,576	$588,155	$653,006	$719,155	$786,626	
BTER								$11,230,537	
Total Cash Flows	-$7,599,263	$401,132	$462,243	$524,576	$588,155	$653,006	$719,155	$12,017,163	
Net Present Value (NPV) @ 10%	$837,614								
Internal Rate of Return (BTIRR)	12.11%								
Return on Cost	6.32%								

pleting the horizontal development and selling the finished parcels to other entities. Overall project returns are shown in table 7-4.

The upper portion of table 7-4 shows the net proceeds from site sales. The apartments and for-sale multifamily residential will account for almost 1 million square feet, almost 60 percent, of the proposed development. The net sales price of $77.7 million reflects a 23 percent margin over horizontal development costs. The remaining construction loan balance and interest accumulated on the construction loan are repaid, leaving equity reversion of $29.6 million. The hotel site re-

turns $3.9 million, and the 27 single-family lots, which sell for an average of $150,000, return $3.8 million. These three amounts enter the spreadsheet in years 2, 3, and 4 respectively.

Investment performance includes the entire equity, which reflects the land value of the 70 acres, cash flows from operating the income-generating properties, and net proceeds from site sales after the construction loan balance is paid. The overall IRR is 17.90 percent for the entire project. The present value of all future cash flows discounted at 10 percent is $53 million.

TABLE 7-3. INFILL REDEVELOPMENT PROJECT INVESTMENT ANAYLSIS FOR INCOME-GENERATING USES

OFFICE DEVELOPMENT	YEARS								
	0	1	2	3	4	5	6	7	8
Gross Potential Revenue		$6,012,900	$6,133,158	$6,255,821	$6,380,938	$6,508,556	$6,638,727	$6,771,502	$6,906,932
– Vacancy Allowance		$721,548	$735,979	$750,699	$765,713	$781,027	$796,647	$812,580	$828,832
Effective Gross Income		$5,291,352	$5,397,179	$5,505,123	$5,615,225	$5,727,530	$5,842,080	$5,958,922	$6,078,100
– Operating Expenses		$1,113,500	$1,135,770	$1,158,485	$1,181,655	$1,205,288	$1,229,394	$1,253,982	$1,279,061
Real Estate Taxes		$334,050	$340,731	$347,546	$354,497	$361,586	$368,818	$376,195	$383,718
NOI		$3,843,802	$3,920,678	$3,999,092	$4,079,073	$4,160,655	$4,243,868	$4,328,745	$4,415,320
less Debt Service		$2,504,390	$2,504,390	$2,504,390	$2,504,390	$2,504,390	$2,504,390	$2,504,390	
Before-Tax Cash Flow		$1,339,412	$1,416,288	$1,494,702	$1,574,683	$1,656,265	$1,739,478	$1,824,355	
Debt-Service Coverage Ratio—Office		1.53	1.57	1.60	1.63	1.66	1.69	1.73	
Gross Sales Price								$51,944,944	
– Selling Expenses								$3,116,697	
Net Sales Price								$48,828,248	
– Unpaid Mortgage Balance								$33,872,739	
Before-Tax Equity Reversion								$14,955,509	
INVESTMENT PERFORMANCE									
Equity	-$11,826,379								
Before-Tax Cash Flow		$1,339,412	$1,416,288	$1,494,702	$1,574,683	$1,656,265	$1,739,478	$1,824,355	
Before-Tax Equity Reversion								$14,955,509	
Total Cash Flows	-$11,826,379	$1,339,412	$1,416,288	$1,494,702	$1,574,683	$1,656,265	$1,739,478	$16,779,864	
NPV @ 10%	$3,073,908								
Before-Tax IRR	15.33%								
Return on Cost	7.65%								

The information for tables 7-3 and 7-4 can be gathered from local and national sources. Real estate brokers are the best source for current information on rents, vacancies, and operating expenses. National sources provide this information for metro markets and subareas within them, as well as information on construction and leasing. CoStar has very good geographic coverage for retail, office, and industrial properties.[5] Developers, brokers, market analysts, and appraisers can offer suggestions for growth rates and capitalization rates. Integra Realty Resources publishes an annual report, "IRR-Viewpoint,"

that includes financial information on 14 property types for 60 large urban areas.[6] For each combination of place and property type, going-in capitalization rate, going-out capitalization rate, rent growth, expense growth, and several other indicators are reported. If you are not located in one of these areas, you can use the all-city averages as general benchmarks.

Community Response to Original Proposal

The concept plan design was prepared by the developer's team without

TABLE 7-4. OVERALL INFILL REDEVELOPMENT PROJECT INVESTMENT ANALYSIS

MULTIFAMILY RESIDENTIAL								
Gross Sales Price	$82,618,362							
– Selling Expenses	$4,957,102							
Net Sales Price	$77,661,260							
– Unpaid Loan Balance	$46,104,563							
– Accumulated Interest	$1,982,819							
Before-Tax Equity Reversion	$29,573,878							
HOTEL								
Gross Sales Price	$4,100,000							
– Selling Expenses	$246,000							
Net Sales Price	$3,854,000							
– Unpaid Loan Balance	$0							
Before-Tax Equity Reversion	$3,854,000							
SINGLE-FAMILY RESIDENTIAL								
Gross Sales Price	$4,050,000	27 lots @ $150,000						
– Selling Expenses	$243,000							
Net Sales Price	$3,807,000							
– Unpaid Loan Balance	$0							
Before-Tax Equity Reversion	$3,807,000							

INVESTMENT PERFORMANCE	YEARS							
	0	**1**	**2**	**3**	**4**	**5**	**6**	**7**
Equity	($41,804,532)							
Before-Tax Cash Flow and Equity Reversion—Retail		$401,132	$462,243	$524,576	$588,155	$653,006	$719,155	$12,017,163
Before-Tax Cash Flow and Equity Reversion—Office		$1,339,412	$1,416,288	$1,494,702	$1,574,683	$1,656,265	$1,739,478	$16,779,864
Before-Tax Equity Reversion from Land Development			$29,573,878	$3,854,000	$3,807,000			
Total Cash Flows	-$41,804,532	$1,740,544	$31,452,409	$5,873,277	$5,969,839	$2,309,271	$2,458,633	$29,797,027
NPV @ 10%	$10,782,550							
Internal Rate of Return (BTIRR)	17.90%							

participation by the residents of either the existing rental units within the project or residents of the adjacent residential neighborhood. When the plan became public, a furor erupted. Residents stated that the project was too dense and too tall, proposed too much parking, and did not respect the need for the type of modest rental housing contained in the existing development. The residents of the adjacent neighborhood, led by the wife of the town mayor, protested, and the issue became a political hot potato.

The neighbors organized and submitted petitions signed by more than 50 percent of the property owners to the town council requesting that the area be designated as a Neighborhood Conservation District (NCD). The NCD classification is applied to a designated neighborhood as a "zoning overlay" that contains land-use regulations specific to that neighborhood. The designation is applied in addition to the underlying use district. It is used to protect distinctive neighborhood characteristics in areas that contribute significantly to the overall character and identity of a town but may lack sufficient historical, architectural, or cultural significance to be designated as Historic Districts. The process to initiate designation consists of two phases: 1) a town-sponsored public information meeting, and 2) a planning board feasibility review and town council action. Once designation is complete, the planning board or an appointed committee develops a neighborhood conservation plan that sets forth design standards. All property owners within the proposed NCD are eligible to participate in drafting the plan, which is then approved as a zoning amendment.

Rather than acting on the developer's application, the town council decided to consider designating the existing development as an NCD. In essence, this referred the dispute to a broader public participation process aimed at building consensus over acceptable development standards. The developer subsequently withdrew his application and agreed to participate in the NCD process. This process acted as the public involvement process for further consideration of the infill project, with leadership from the town's planning staff and representation from all affected interests. On council instructions, an outside facilitator was hired. The facilitator structured the process to facilitate a constructive dialogue between the property owners and the neighbors, beyond the typical public information meeting. At the successful conclusion of the first phase, in 2009, the feasibility review proceeded.

The council established an NCD committee comprised of neighborhood residents, apartment tenants, developer's representatives, a representative of the neighboring church, and others. Over the course of some 28 meetings in two years, this committee carried out an intensive feasibility review process. It concluded in 2012 with the issuance and formal adoption of the Neighborhood Conservation District Plan. This three-part plan set specific standards for the area of the proposed redevelopment project, as well as for the adjacent neighborhoods. The developer was then able to prepare a second design based on the adopted NCD standards.

During the feasibility review process carried out by the NCD committee, the goal was to learn the underlying interests of all the stakeholders. For example, it became clear that preservation of the character of the existing neighborhood, which featured numerous trees and gently curving streets with undulating frontages, was a more important concern to the current neighbors and residents than particular buildings or densities. This guided the developer's design team to place buildings around existing street trees, create pockets of open space where existing cottages were located, and maintain the existing street network rather than trying to straighten out individual street segments. Taking time to educate one another on their joint interests helped the participants to improve the quality of the plan and the potential success of the future development.

After listening to everyone's interests, the developer put together a list of development principles that were important to the community and that the developer was willing to use to guide the project design. This list was reviewed and accepted by the committee. It stated:

Redevelopment Guiding Principles
- Value the history of the neighborhood.
- Preserve the street network.

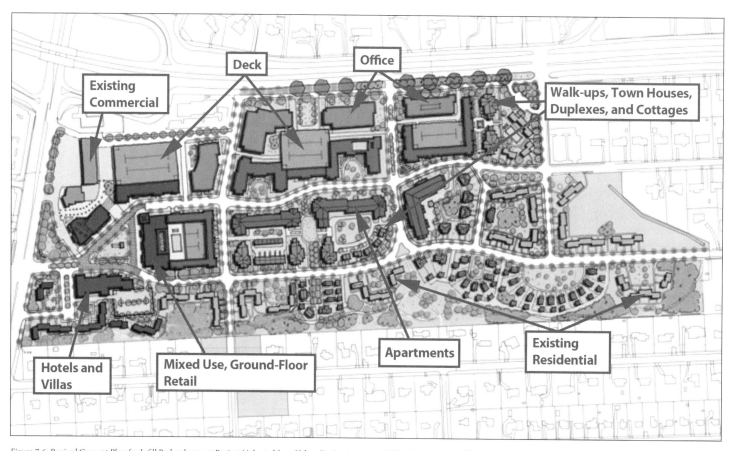

Figure 7-6. Revised Concept Plan for Infill Redevelopment Project (Adapted from Urban Design Associates, 2012. Courtesy of Grubb Properties and Urban Design Associates.)

- Create and maintain open space.
- Preserve existing trees.
- Maintain a portion of the buildings.
- Transition and vary density and heights.
- Buffer adjacent residences.
- Preserve the church's visibility and accessibility.
- Generate an effective transportation strategy.
- Increase sustainability.

- Promote community diversity.

The developer then created a revised concept plan based on these principles. He presented it to the committee in stages, getting feedback, going back to the drawing board, and developing subsequent plan proposals. Putting the principles into concept drawings and presenting them visually helped to illustrate the impact of the principles and assisted the committee in arriving at

Figure 7-7. Pedestrian Realm Rendering. (Urban Design Associates, 2012. Courtesy of Grubb Properties and Urban Design Associates.)

TABLE 7-5. REVISED PROPOSED USES	
USE TYPES	**NUMBERS**
Single-Family Residential	94 units
Cottages	26 units
Duplexes	56 units
Town Houses	12 units
Multifamily Residential	405 units
Apartments	125 units
For-sale	280 units
Hotel	175 rooms
Main Building	150 rooms
Villas	25 rooms
Retail	76,032 SF
Existing	26,032 SF
New	50,000 SF
Office	300,000 SF
Parking Total	1,672 spaces
Decked	1,330 spaces
Surface	342 spaces

a consensus plan. After long discussions, the developer's proposed plans were completed. Then the town hired a third-party firm to hold a visioning workshop, and the developer brought in a design consultant to finalize the concept plan, based on the committee's feedback. (See figure 7-6.)

Revised Development Proposal

The revised design rethought the proposed density, height, and parking. It changed the land-use patterns by placing office buildings on the west side facing U.S. 15-501, moving the parking decks toward the west, keeping the existing commercial on N.C. 54, and putting mixed use with ground-floor retail at the main entrance, along with a hotel and associated villas. It maintained a buffer of existing residential and green space, along with small-scale cottages and town houses, adjacent to the existing neighborhood to the east. Its larger multifamily buildings were located in the center of the site. (See figure 7-7.)

Along with the site plan, the mix of uses and intensities was modified substantially. Based on the revised concept plan, the first-cut development program set out ranges of potential amounts of housing, office, and retail square footage. The ranges were to be firmed up in the process of creating the final development program to be submitted for review and approval by the town. At this stage,

the NCD participants were more concerned about the types and locations of uses and circulation patterns than about specific densities, which had not been completely determined, leaving some latitude in the development plan.

For the purposes of this financial analysis, we assumed a first-cut set of densities that were consistent with the revised site plan. Table 7-5 shows these assumed densities, which were used to test the financial feasibility of the revised project. In reality, additional revised project scenarios would be examined. The most significant changes with this alternative are: 1) conservation of 80–90 apartment units instead of development of a new single-family area, 2) maintenance of the existing street pattern, 3) reduction of both structured and surface parking, 4) reduction of building mass to create more openness and less impervious surface area, and 5) refurbishment of the existing retail and addition of new retail in that area.

Financial Analysis of Revised Infill Redevelopment Proposal

The original project proposal was submitted in 2008. The revised proposal is likely to be finalized in 2013, with construction beginning in 2014. If our objective was to present an accurate case study, we would examine the economic and financial implications of changes that resulted from the development agreement and new physical design five years after the initial proposal. We would update rents, expenses, development costs, and underwriting criteria. Such a before-and-after comparison would underscore a very salient point about real estate development: although conventional wisdom points out the importance of "location, location, location," wise developers know that successful development requires the right "timing, timing, timing." If the plan had been approved in 2008, relatively high prerecession development costs would have been incurred to build this project, which would have then been marketed during the recession. The project could have failed. Certainly, financial return expectations would not have been met. The delay may enable the developer to build at relatively low costs and rent or sell into a rising market. Good timing may have trumped great location.

However, we have a different objective than examining the economic and financial implications of changes to the plan five years after the initial proposal. We want to show the financial impacts of the revised project using exactly the same cost-revenue and financing structure as in the original case. In this way, we can estimate the financial implications of the regulations and new site plan, all things being equal. Therefore, our financial analysis for the revised project replicates the calculations completed for the original project proposal, with the same unit costs and revenues. We ask if the revised concept plan would have been feasible to develop if it were to be built starting in 2014.

The revised project is less intense than the original proposal. It involves less land, demolition, site development, parking, and construction. Financing costs are lower. Soft costs are doubled to account for

TABLE 7-6. COMPARISON OF ORIGINAL PROPOSAL TO REVISED PROPOSAL FOR THE INFILL PROJECT

	Original Proposal	Revised Proposal
Overall Internal Rate of Return (IRR)	17.90%	6.53%
Net Present Value (NPV) at 10% Discount Rate	$10,782,550	$4,728,113
Internal Rate of Return (IRR)—Retail	12.11%	3.06%
Internal Rate of Return (IRR)—Office	15.33%	7.15%
Total Development Cost	$167,087,582	$129,656,540
Retail Development	$48,339,730	$11,873,583
Office Development	$50,264,399	$64,123,146
Equity Investment	$41,804,532	$35,832,456

the extended negotiation period, additional studies, and use of outside consultants. The property types remain the same. The amount of single-family residential, office, and hotel uses increase, whereas multifamily residential and retail decrease substantially.

The capital budgets, investment analyses for the income-generating property, and overall project performance were revised to account for all changes. The results comparing the original infill redevelopment project to the revised project are summarized in table 7-6.

The analysis shows that the returns for the revised proposal are less than for the original proposal. This decrease translates into returns that are far too low to make the project financially feasible. The overall IRR drops by over 10 percentage points. As a result, the NPV of the project discounted at 10 percent goes from $10.8 million positive to $4.7 million negative.

Internal rates of return for retail and office development reflect these overall results. Retail IRR drops to 3.06 percent, from the original proposal's IRR of 12.11 percent. Office IRR drops by more than half, to 7.15 percent.

In the original proposal, the developer invests $41.8 million in equity to produce a project that costs $167.1 million. Returns on this investment are reasonable. In the revised proposal, $35.8 million in equity is used for a project that costs $129.7 million. Returns in the revised proposal are unacceptably low. This is a clear indication that the project must go back to the drawing board and that basic development, design, and regulatory assumptions need to be reassessed. The politically acceptable infill project is not sufficiently profitable to be built under the 2008 scenario. Without more intense redevelopment, all potential sustainability gains will be lost.

Pushing the Envelope for Sustainability

How should designers, developers, and planners respond to this infeasible outcome? Designers can focus on the physical dimension, the site plan, and infrastructure. They might try to increase the density of the residential buildings in the center of the site. Density can often be increased in minimally obtrusive ways through creative design. The town houses, walk-up units, and some duplexes might be replaced with more-intense residential uses, as the reduction from 745 to 405 multifamily units had the greatest negative impact on financial returns. Rethinking the layout of the residential areas might suggest some less expensive ways of dealing with parking, including shared off-peak parking arrangements. Designers might also introduce green infrastructure in the form of streets, stormwater management, and natural energy into their plans, which could reduce long-term operating costs (see Sarté 2010).

Developers can focus on the economic dimension. They might review the mix of possible uses to determine if more-profitable options exist. Perhaps seniors housing, specialized life-science-oriented lab space, or a medical or veterinary office may be needed in the market, and these could generate attractive financial returns. The villas associated with the hotel could be expanded and marketed to an extended-stay hospitality provider. Developers might also review the cost and technology assumptions in the capital budget. For example, parking options may exist that could drive down the unit cost of the parking decks. Finally, developers could explore the payoff potential of various green building options that would reduce future operating costs.

Planners can focus on the legal and regulatory dimension. They might try to find ways to increase the intensity and density of the project through changes in zoning regulations and design standards. They might try to maintain the best features of the revised site plan and suggest modifications that would increase floor area ratios. They might provide incentives for increasing sustainability, such as fast-track permit and zoning reviews that would decrease the costs of time delays. Planners also might advocate a form-based zoning approach that facilitates urban design consensus building at the start of development rather than a drawn-out process of negotiating the form and details of each new project revision.[7]

One further option would be to have the public sector subsidize the project to make it more financially attractive. Although this is not an uncommon approach, the resulting project would clearly be more costly to the public and might be less sustainable than more compact, intense alternatives that meet the test of market and financial feasibility. Community resistance to compact infill redevelopment should motivate developers, designers, and planners to work together effectively to propose even more compelling sustainable projects.

Summary: Infill Redevelopment Alternatives

Mixed use infill development projects are more complex and challenging than single-use and greenfield projects. Because of their longer time horizons and more complex financial arrangements, these infill projects are best understood with the use of dynamic financial analysis, which captures the projected flow of transactions that occur from the start of a project to its conclusion.

This chapter applies dynamic financial analysis to the redevelopment of an older 70-acre site containing rental apartments and a small retail center into a contemporary mixed use infill project. Converting the original low-density, suburban-style rental housing into a more intense mix of housing, retail, and office with supporting parking proved to be a difficult and time-consuming process, due to a firestorm of neighborhood opposition to the increased density and change of character. However, after a two-year collaborative process, the developer and the neighbors were able to reach consensus on a new set of development principles and a revised concept plan that changed the layout, reduced the density, and preserved much of the original character. That's the good news: the NCD overlay zoning process worked to bring the parties together.

The bad news, at least as identified through our illustrative application of dynamic financial analysis to the original and revised project plans, is that the new concept plan may not be financially feasible. In the original proposal, the developer invests $41.8 million in equity to produce a project that costs $167.1 million. Returns on this investment are reasonable. According to our assumptions about the revised proposal, $35.8 million in equity is used for a project that costs $129.7 million. Returns in the revised proposal are unacceptably low. This indicates that the project must go back to the drawing board and that basic development, design, and regulatory elements must be reassessed. The politically acceptable infill project does not appear sufficiently profitable to be built. Without more intense redevelopment, all potential sustainability gains could be lost.

What could be done to respond to this infeasible outcome? Designers might try to increase the density of the residential buildings in the center of the site, replacing the town houses, walk-up units, and duplexes with more-intense residential uses, since the reduction from 745 to 405 multifamily units had the greatest negative impact on financial returns. They might also rethink the parking, including considering shared off-peak parking arrangements, and might introduce green streets and stormwater management, and natural energy provision.

Developers might review the mix of possible uses in the program to determine if more-profitable options exist, such as seniors housing, extended-stay villas, specialized lab space, or a medical or veterinary office. They might also review less expensive parking options and look for green building possibilities that would reduce future operating costs.

Planners might try to find ways to increase the intensity and density of the project through changes in zoning regulations and design standards, as well as fast-track permit and zoning reviews that would decrease the costs of time delays. They might recommend a form-based zoning approach that facilitates consensus building at the start of development rather than a drawn-out negotiation over the form of each new project revision.

Finally, developers and planners might work together to explore the feasibility of using public subsidies to offset some development costs in order to assist in generating the desired public benefits to be derived from the consensus project design. Grants for affordable housing, green infrastructure, or structured parking are possibilities, as are tax incentives or special financing districts linked to development agreements.

Clearly, infill redevelopment that is compact, connected, and mixed use is more sustainable than sprawl development. The original redevelopment alternative for the 70-acre property offered reasonable public benefits and private returns. The revised alternative satisfied the neighbors but was not financially feasible. Designers, developers, and planners need to find a third alternative that satisfies the agreed-upon guiding principles, generates acceptable financial returns, and advances sustainability.

Urban Village, Lowertown, Saint Paul, Minnesota

MASTER DEVELOPER: Lowertown Redevelopment Corporation

WEBSITE: Website: www.lowertown.org

Led by President Weiming Lu, the independent Lowertown Redevelopment Corporation (LRC) forged a new vision for this abandoned warehouse area of Saint Paul. For two decades, LRC carried out a revitalization campaign that balanced historic preservation and redevelopment. It focused on urban design; providing marketing and creative (gap) financing to implement projects and plans; and pursuing sustainability by adapting existing resources, buildings, and infrastructure, and advocating light-rail transit. Walkable neighborhoods, district heating, locally grown foods, and reclamation of brownfields were implemented. Established with a $10 million McKnight Foundation Program-Related Investment (loan fund), it attracted some $750 million in new investments through public-private partnerships by 2006 and another $250 million from the subsequent Union Depot restoration. A $957 million light-rail transit system will connect it with downtown Minneapolis in 2014. Winner of a Presidential Design Award, Lowertown is a thriving community of new housing, artists' studios, "cyber villagers" (internet service and content providers), supercomputer and biomedical firms, and public parks and open spaces. Rather than a single development project, Lowertown is a sustainable urban village designed by numerous architects, bringing together a host of initiatives into a lively neighborhood (Lu 2013).

From top to bottom: Figure 8-1. Lowertown Building Exterior (Courtesy of Lowertown Redevelopment Corporation.); Figure 8-2. Urban Village Plan of Lowertown, Saint Paul, Minnesota (Courtesy of Bentz/Thompson/Rietow Architects of Minneapolis.)

Urban Village Plan
as a guide for redevelopment

New housing and winter garden

District heating, observe energy codes, protect solar access, and other energy conservation measures

Adaptive reuse of historic buildings

Improve parks, streetscape, and extend skyways to the area

Build cyber village, improve infrastructure for old and new economy

Multimodal station at Union Depot for light-rail transit, commuter rail and Amtrak

Build artist housing, space for artists and arts organization

Reclaim riverfront for housing, plaza, winter garden, and marina

Reclaim an abandoned rail yard as the Bruce Vento Nature Sanctuary and connect regional trails

Chapter 8

Development Coordination Recommendations

Development projects can contribute to urban sustainability. The amount of their contribution varies with the scale and type of project. Our three cases have considered projects of different types and scales, each with its own contributions: an apartment infill case, a greenfield residential subdivision case, and an infill redevelopment case.

Lessons from Three Types of Urban Projects

The apartment infill case in chapters 3 and 4 seeks to place a new urban-type complex on a 12.5-acre property in a built-up urban area. By making use of a vacant parcel already served by urban infrastructure and transit, the apartment infill project adds residential density without expanding the borders of the urban area, thereby avoiding sprawl. It offers residential accommodations for households working in the metro area. The selected site plan recognizes the existence of a floodplain and protects this environmental resource area with a surrounding buffer. Overall, the project provides a modest, but clear, contribution to sustainability.

The greenfield subdivision case in chapter 5 seeks to develop a residential subdivision on a 36-acre property adjacent to an existing 95-acre subdivision. While the project is outside the municipal boundaries, it is within the urban transition area; makes use of existing water and sewer services; is compatible with its residential context; and adds green features, such as a community garden. Its site plan also protects the floodplain on the property, turning the lake into a community amenity. By maximizing the project density within the limits of the development regulations, the design concentrates additional single-family housing adjacent to an existing neighborhood. Overall, the project's contribution to sustainability, while not as substantial as that of multifamily housing inside the town limits, is a reasonable response to existing conditions of land use and ownership patterns.

The infill redevelopment case in chapter 7 seeks to transform an existing apartment neighborhood from the post–World War II era into a contemporary project that includes housing, office, and retail uses on a 70-acre site. Located inside a municipality and adjacent to an older single-family neighborhood, this adaptive reuse effort reflects the advantages of, and the obstacles to, larger-scale infill redevelopment. Advantages include the ability to reuse existing street patterns; fit into a mature landscape; connect to roads, transit, and infrastructure; and provide larger amounts of accessible housing and commercial uses in an integrated design. Obstacles include the extra time and effort necessary to gain agreement on the plan among stakeholders, the more complex financing arrangements, and the more difficult government approval process. Given the potential advantages, along with the opportunities to overcome the obstacles, this type of project clearly offers the most substantial contributions to urban sustainability. It makes positive use of existing urban resources, allows for a process of building neighborhood agreement on the nature of change, and does not contribute to urban sprawl.

Design, $, Rules

Lessons from the infill redevelopment case highlight the need for a publicly sanctioned process of consensus building over the nature and impacts of a proposed project. On the one hand, large-scale redevelopment is necessary if a project is to significantly reduce sprawl. On the other hand, the larger a project and its associated impacts, the more difficult it is to resolve neighborhood disputes about the plan. On the one hand, to modernize and adapt existing buildings and streets, it is necessary to demolish some existing structures and change the nature of the environment. On the other hand, the more demolition and change that is planned, the more difficult and expensive it is to satisfy existing tenants of the project site and to meet environmental and development regulations. On the one hand, the potential profit from a large-scale project is likely to attract more-substantial investment resources. On the other hand, the complex nature of redevelopment makes it more difficult to demonstrate to investors that the returns outweigh the risks. The list goes on; the point is that the bigger a project's contribution to urban sustainability, the larger the changes it requires. Large-scale urban redevelopment infill projects promise great leaps forward for urban sustainability, but they demand strong working relationships among developers, planners, and designers.

Collaborative Development

The preceding chapters demonstrate how designers, developers, and planners can break through their professional silos and work together more effectively. The outcomes come closer to the ideal of comprehensive planning in the sense that all relevant perspectives are taken into account. It would be simpler, no doubt, to allow these groups to dominate their own aspects of the development process. Designers might create attractive urban form, developers might achieve impressive financial returns, and planners might celebrate the public benefits of implemented plans. Yet in the real world of conflicting objectives and differential power, the best outcomes are ones that achieve trade-offs acceptable to all parties.

Designers and planners share many values and tend to agree on projects that would help create sustainable places to live, work, and play. They are well versed in the physical, and legal and institutional, dimensions of development but less so in development economics and financial analysis. Developers are more concerned about the market for, and the financial implications of, their projects. Savvy developers recognize that they are producing space (contents) in buildings (containers) to satisfy two distinct markets: the space users who will buy or rent the contents, and the neighbors and public at large who will have to live with the containers for many, many years. They should produce better projects for both markets if they work successfully with designers and planners who understand the market and financial dimensions of development. The static and dynamic tools of financial analysis presented in previous chapters should facilitate better understanding among developers, designers, and planners.

Opportunities for Creating Sustainable Projects

Each type of actor in the development triangle presented at the start of this book has an opportunity to contribute to project sustainability. Developers can envision feasible projects that not only return acceptable profits but also incorporate best practices in green building and walkable neighborhoods. Designers can envision beautiful projects that not only represent high-quality site planning and architecture but also meet community standards and are financially feasible. And planners can envision sustainable projects based on regulatory standards that not only implement the goals of community plans but also relate design and development proposals to the broader mandates of the public interest.

Because they set the rules of the game, planners can play a particularly important role in determining project sustainability. What can planners do to encourage sustainable projects? As seen from the illustrative examples, development regulations are major determinants of project feasibility. New types of regulations aimed at creating sustainable communities seek to overcome problems found in traditional ordinances. Planners can preview the impacts of such new regulations by applying them to the types of development desired in the comprehensive plan. Rather than viewing

1 Introduction
2. Environmental Health and Natural Resources
    2.1. Climate Change
    2.2. Low Impact Development and Green Infrastructure
    2.3. Natural Resource Conservation / Sensitive Lands Protection
    2.4. Water Conservation
    2.5. Solid Waste and Recycling
3. Natural Hazards
    3.1. Floodplain Management
    3.2. Wildfires in the Wildland-Urban Interface
    3.3. Coastal Hazards
    3.4. Steep Slopes
4. Land Use and Community Character
    4.1. Character and Aesthetics
    4.2. Urban Form and Density
    4.3. Historic Preservation
5. Mobility and Transportation
    5.1. Transit Oriented Development
    5.2. Mobility Systems
        5.2.1. Complete Streets
        5.2.2. Bicycle Mobility Systems
        5.2.3 Pedestrian Mobility Systems
    5.3. Public Transit
    5.4. Parking
6. Community
    6.1. Community Development
    6.2. Public Participation and Community Benefits
7. Healthy Neighborhoods, Housing, Food Security
    7.1. Community Health and Safety
    7.2. Affordable Housing
    7.3. Housing Diversity and Accessibility
    7.4. Food Production and Security
8. Energy
    8.1. Renewable Energy: Wind (small- and large-scale)
    8.2. Renewable Energy: Solar (including solar access)
    8.3. Energy Efficiency and Conservation
9. Livability
    9.1. Noise
    9.2. Lighting
    9.3. Visual Elements

Figure 8-3. Table of Contents, Sustainable Community Development Code Framework (Rocky Mountain Land Use Institute, www.law.du.edu/index.php/rmlui/rmlui-practice/code-framework.)

themselves as aloof regulators, planners can work collaboratively with developers and designers.

For example, the Sustainable Community Development Code Framework created by the Rocky Mountain Land Use Institute contains specific regulations relating to climate change, low-impact development and green infrastructure, natural resource conservation and sensitive lands protection, and other topics (see figure 8-3). It seeks to offer incentives for, reduce obstacles to, and set standards for, sustainable development.

If some of these regulations had been tested against our illustrative examples, they could have identified opportunities to improve design and development while increasing project sustainability. For example, the Sustainable Community Development Code Framework recommends allowing, by right, mixed use development, accessory units, and live-work units in residential zone districts. It also recommends allowing the tailoring of development standards to encourage infill and mixed use development by allowing plazas, community gardens, and green roofs to count as alternative open space. If these alternatives had been tested in our apartment and residential subdivision cases, they could have shown how to make better use of the project sites and to increase the flexibility and intensity of the proposed designs. In transit-oriented development districts, the code framework suggests reducing processing fees, expediting the review process, and specifying maximum parking standards. Given that the mixed use infill example case could be configured as a transit-oriented development, these incentives and standards could have guided more-sustainable project alternatives.

Financial Analysis at Higher Levels of Planning

As noted in chapter 1, planners engage in comprehensive planning at the urban scale; small-area planning for specific neighborhoods, districts, or corridors; and planning at the project level that primarily involves the application of regulatory standards to the review of development projects. Previous chapters demonstrate how financial analysis can be used at the project level. What about at these higher levels of planning?

Comprehensive Planning

Comprehensive planning is implemented through regulation and public spending. The former involves creating the official map and enforcing zoning. The latter involves updating the capital improvements program to include infrastructure and public facility projects over the next 5–10 years. Local public improvements in the period from the end of World War II until 1980 were primarily financed with public funds from all levels of government. Indeed, the federal government was the primary source of funding for highways and water and sewer projects. Local governments relied on general obligation bonds to fund schools, parks, and other public facilities that were open to the public. Local utilities used revenue bonds to fund facilities that could be repaid with dedicated sources of revenue.

The funding environment changed radically around 1980. For many reasons, local jurisdictions were hard-pressed to find adequate resources for public infrastructure and facilities. The poor condition of much of the infrastructure in the United States today is the consequence. New tools have been fashioned to finance growth. Some have been used as incentives for economic development, whereas others are designed to accommodate development impacts.

Although state and federal grants and loan programs still exist, most funding now comes from local sources. The popular financing techniques include: 1) financing based on property value increases resulting from development, 2) financing based on the off-site impacts of development, and 3) public-private partnerships.

The first category includes special assessment districts and tax increment financing. Both require estimation of the property values within a defined area before and after the infrastructure improvements are made. The value increment becomes the revenue source to pay for any revenue bonds issued to finance the infrastructure.

Impact fees are the most typical way to pay for the impacts that development projects have on the community at large. The fees are paid by developers or home builders to cover the burden imposed on specific forms of public infrastructure, such as roads, schools, and parks. The level of fees reflects application of the rational nexus test.

Impact taxes, concurrency requirements, and adequate public facility ordinances take a similar approach.

Public-private partnerships use a wide range of financing approaches. They have been created to provide public facilities and infrastructure in many areas, including water and sewer, transportation, technology infrastructure, public works, schools, health care facilities, energy, and environmental projects. The National Council for Public-Private Partnerships tracks these relationships.[1]

Small-Area Planning

Planning for subareas of jurisdictions has become more common since the 1990s, as urban or city design has regained importance in the urban planning field. These plans are often initiated by local planners who want to articulate future development in greater detail. One subset of such plans includes the redevelopment visions generated for central areas, abandoned malls, and brownfield areas, often through community charrettes. Several applications of financial analysis appear attractive at this level of planning: 1) examining tax yields for different areas, 2) comparing different development scenarios, and 3) forecasting the impacts of infrastructure investment on specific small areas.

The basic ideas behind the first application are that urban land values vary significantly, and land development occurs only after public investments. In other words, public infrastructure and facilities turn land into developable sites. Cities benefit when site development is completed by receiving *ad valorem* property taxes and associated sales taxes. To understand differences in land use and land value more completely, planners, finance officers, and assessors should analyze assessed values and related tax yields on a per-acre basis. Tax yields per acre will vary significantly. In some cities, this analysis has been completed to gauge how important the CBD is for tax revenue generation.

The second application can provide planners with a valuable way to compare small-area development scenarios. Because scale will vary, it is important to use the same spatial unit of analysis, which again will

Revenue per Acre

TABLE 8-1. COMPARISON OF PROJECT VERSUS PER-ACRE METRICS

	Suburban Walmart		Downtown Mixed Use	
	Project Level	Per Acre	Project Level	Per Acre
Land Consumed	34 acres		0.2 acres	
Property Taxes	$221,000	$6,500	$126,800	$634,000
City Retail Taxes	$1,615,000	$47,500	$16,720	$83,600
Residents	0	0	18	90
Jobs	200	5.9	15	73.7

Sources: Joe Minicozzi, AICP, Principal, Urban3 (www.urban-three.com), Asheville, North Carolina, and the authors.

be per acre. This application is similar to the first in that it estimates expected tax yields, but it does so for several development scenarios. With this application, the most attractive alternative can be identified, at least from the public revenue perspective.

This application has significant educational value for local officials, residents, and the development community. They tend to look at development alternatives at the *project* level without examining outcomes *per acre*. As a result, large development alternatives always look better than modest ones.

For example, two development alternatives in Asheville, North Carolina, are compared in table 8-1. The aggregate fiscal and economic impacts of one alternative, a suburban Walmart, overwhelm those of the other, a mixed use downtown infill. At the project level, the Walmart pays substantially more taxes and generates many more jobs. But the results change dramatically when the two alternatives are compared using the proper metric.

The Walmart uses 170 times more land than the mixed use project. This huge difference in land consumption explains why the infill project has superior fiscal and economic returns per acre. The analysis could be expanded to account for differences in infrastructure costs, parking, and land values. But the results would still underscore the importance of using the correct metric, which should promote better stewardship of urban land.

Finally, the public infrastructure investments associated with small-area plans can be examined to gauge their potential to generate tax revenues. The most straightforward approach to showing the increase in tax revenues expected to come from the small area is to compare existing conditions to those expected to exist once the infrastructure is in place. The zoning based on the small-area plan provides the best guide for future development and can be used to anticipate land uses and density. SketchUp models can be drawn to make a before-and-after comparison in three dimensions. The results will estimate return on infrastructure investment and the associated risk. This risk-return analysis can be applied to any small area destined to receive new infrastructure or upgrades. It can also be used to compare the public return on infrastructure investment for a number of different small areas, to help identify those that promise the highest return on public investment. This final application of financial analysis is explained fully in the appendix to this chapter.

Conclusion

Planners need to understand the design and development issues inherent in their proposed comprehensive plans and development regulations. Designers need to understand the financial issues inherent in the project plans they create. And developers need to understand the design and planning issues inherent in their project programs. A collaborative approach bringing these groups together can build understanding and lead to more-sustainable project proposals.

Our final recommendation is for each type of actor in the project planning and development arena to "walk a mile in the other's moccasins." The insights gained by reversing roles can not only raise the quality of design, development, and regulation, but can also create a more open and collaborative process of city design in which the players work together to build sustainable communities.

Appendix to Chapter 8

Methods for gauging the return on infrastructure investment for areas within jurisdictions are presented in this appendix. A jurisdiction installs or upgrades infrastructure to facilitate property development, which, in turn, adds to the jurisdiction's tax base and generates annual property tax payments. The public investment is the cost of new infrastructure. The return on this public investment is the present value of future property tax revenues generated from the additional tax base. The method to calculate expected returns is presented first, followed by the method suggested to assess risk. The headings represent the steps involved, and the commentaries elaborate on them.

Return on Investment Method

Time Horizon

- Select an appropriate time period associated with the small-area plan, say 20 years.

Current Taxes Paid

- Create a spreadsheet listing all parcels included in the small-area plan.
- Include current information on land use, intensity of use, whether it is taxed or tax exempt, assessed value, and property taxes currently paid.
- Compute the total property tax revenues currently generated.

Build-Out Scenario

- Show the anticipated development in the small area categorized by land use and intensity of use.
- Insert this information in the spreadsheet parcel by parcel.

Forecasts of Households and Employment

- Find the most credible forecasts of population (by place of residence) and employment (by place of work) for the selected time horizon.

- Formulate a defensible way to allocate population growth to the small area.
- Use information on trends in household size to transform the population forecast into a forecast of the number of households.
- Rely on economic development professionals to estimate employment for the small area given the employment forecast for the entire urban area.

Forecasts of Space Occupancy

- Assume that each household will occupy one dwelling unit.
- Find historical data on occupancy for office and retail space for at least 10 years.
- Find historical employment data for the same time period.
- Regress occupancy on employment to estimate a regression equation.
- Use the equation to find the amount of occupied space for the forecast amount of employment.

Forecasts of Dwelling Units and Gross Building Area

- Consult with real estate professionals to generate estimates of normal vacancy rates of residential and commercial property.
- Calculate each occupancy rate, which is one minus the vacancy rate, giving the percentage of full occupancy.
- Find an estimate of the efficiency ratio applicable to office and retail property. (The efficiency ratio is the quotient of net rentable area to gross building area.)
- Divide the number of dwelling units by the residential occupancy rate to get the total number of dwelling units for the small area.
- Divide the amount of occupied commercial space by the occupancy rate to find total rentable area.
- Then divide total rentable area of commercial space by the efficiency ratio(s) to find the amount of gross building area for the small area.

Comparison of Dwelling Unit and Commercial Space Forecasts to Expected Development at Build-Out

- Compare the number of dwelling units and amount of commercial space at build-out in the spreadsheet to the forecasts of dwelling units and commercial space generated for the time horizon.
- Use the forecasts of dwelling units and commercial space for the remainder of this analysis.

Forecast Value of Dwelling Units and Commercial Development

- Select an appropriate average cost per dwelling unit in the small area.
- Multiply this average by the number of forecast dwelling units to find the total value of housing.
- Consult with general contractors and real estate developers to estimate the cost of commercial space per square foot.
- Multiply this average by the amount of gross building area to find the total value of commercial space.
- Add the value of dwellings and commercial space together to find the total forecast value of development in the small area.

Estimated Present Value of Forecast Development

- Divide the total forecast value by the time horizon to get annual values.
- After the first year, add the annual values to the previous year's amount until all development value is accounted for by the last year.
- Select an appropriate discount rate.
- Use the selected discount rate to find the present value of the annual property values.

Estimated Return on Investment

- Multiply the present value of forecast development by the current property tax rate to find anticipated tax revenues.

- Subtract the current property tax revenues for the small area from the forecast amount to find the expected increase in property taxes.
- Estimate the current cost of all planned infrastructure in the small area.
- Divide the increase in property taxes by the cost of infrastructure to find return on investment (ROI).

Commentary on Return on Investment Method

Time Horizon

The time horizon should be long enough to realize benefits from infrastructure investments but short enough to include reasonable forecasts of population and employment. Twenty years is a good compromise.

Current Taxes Paid and Build-Out Scenario

The spreadsheet provides the database that is associated with the graphic depictions of the current situation and the build-out scenario.

Forecasts of Households and Employment

The most difficult task is to forecast development for the small area. Even with reliable forecasts of population and employment for the larger urban area, it is very challenging to allocate a growth increment to a specific small area. It is tempting to assume that the employment and household growth shown in the small-area plan will be strong enough to absorb all of the development anticipated at build-out. This assumption means that supply will generate its own demand. This is a version of Say's Law in economics, which was refuted in the 1930s. In fact, it may be more reasonable to assume that employment and household growth will occupy existing vacant commercial and residential space rather than new construction. There is considerable vacant space available in many urban areas as the result of the recent recession.

The household forecast is less difficult, because population growth is primarily determined by the natural increase of the current population, and trends in household size are well documented.

The employment forecast is especially challenging, which is why we recommend you consult local economic development professionals. They should be able to suggest the amount of total employment that could be attracted to the small area. Although subjective, an approach based on expert opinion is more credible than a quantitative method that is easy to apply but much harder to defend.

Economic development professionals may prefer to think in terms of basic and nonbasic employment. Basic employment sectors export goods or services beyond the metro area. Nonbasic sectors serve the local market. With an estimate of basic employment, an appropriate economic-base multiplier is needed to find total employment. This multiplier can come from various sources, but the best source is economic researchers familiar with the local economy.

Forecasts of Space Occupancy
Although the small area may include additional commercial uses, such as industrial (flex space or warehouse space) and lodging, the assumption is that office and retail space will dominate.

The relationship between employment and space use can be estimated using an industry standard such as square feet of space per employee. However, regression analysis should give more accurate results. Historical data are available from CoStar. Local real estate companies that subscribe to this database may be willing to share the historical information. Otherwise, there are local firms that provide real estate data in most urban areas.

Forecasts of Dwelling Units and Gross Building Area
Normal residential and commercial vacancy rates are available from various local and national sources. The commercial rate will be an average for office and retail space. Information on building efficiency can be found from local or national real estate companies. Local construction contractors can also be consulted for reasonable estimates. Retail space is built more efficiently than office space; again, an average for both retail and office space should be used to keep the analysis simple.

Comparison of Dwelling Unit and Commercial Space Forecasts to Expected Development at Build-Out
For several reasons, the build-out scenario is likely to show larger amounts of housing and commercial space than the amounts forecast for the next 20 years. First, the physical conditions in the area rarely generate major constraints on vertical development. Second, the zoning for the small area should correlate with the capacity of the available and proposed infrastructure but will usually allow for generous increases in development. Third, the market, or demand, for space is the factor that usually constrains development. The space forecasts represent the amount of development the market can support for the next 20 years, which is less than build-out. Thus, it will take more than 20 years to achieve build-out given forecast market conditions.

Forecast Value of Dwelling Units and Commercial Development
The simplifying assumption here is that the cost of construction and development can be equated to the value of development. The average housing value includes land value, which is usually about 20 percent of total value. The value of commercial space is more complex, because the amount spent on land acquisition and site development varies by project and area. The best approach is to assign a low percentage to land value, say 10–15 percent, and add that to the cost of vertical development to find the total value of commercial development.

The alternative is to estimate the value of commercial property by analyzing its income-generating potential. Local real estate appraisers could be asked to estimate the value of forecast commercial space. They would use information on rents, vacancies, expenses, capitalization rates, and so on to do the analysis. However, the work would be costly, and the necessary assumptions would be easy to criticize. Thus, the cost approach seems to be the better option.

Estimated Present Value of Forecast Development
Although real estate markets are cyclical, it is reasonable to assume a linear trend when spreading development over the time horizon in

this analysis. The equal increments are added year by year, from the beginning to the end of the time horizon. A long-term real estate cycle could be introduced by varying the amount of annual development above or below the average for the time horizon.

The discount rate reflects the longer time horizon of public investments and would be much lower than those discussed in chapters 6 and 7. Social discount rates are often quoted in the 3–6 percent range. The best option is to use the local jurisdiction's cost-of-funds rate.

Estimated Return on Investment

It is more conservative to assume existing tax rates for the analysis than to assume tax increases. Estimates of infrastructure costs should be available from the city's engineering and public works department. Return on investment is found by dividing the present value of tax revenues by infrastructure costs. Both estimates reflect current dollars.

The return on investment estimate is subject to several important caveats. First, the infrastructure in the small area is likely to last longer than the time horizon used in the analysis. The longer it lasts, the higher the return. However, operation and maintenance expenditures are required to keep the infrastructure functional. As would be done in a fiscal impact analysis, these expenditures could be subtracted from property tax revenues, which would lower return on investment.

The analysis could be made more complex by incorporating sales tax revenues resulting from the new commercial development. Sales taxes would be paid by residents patronizing retailers, and visitors staying at lodging facilities in the small area. The local share of sales taxes received over time would increase return on investment.

Risk Assessment

Return on investment depends primarily on the amount of population and employment the small area can capture over the time horizon. Risk can be effectively assessed by calculating two other sets of capture rates. The first set is based on the unrealistic assumption that growth will fill the entire development envelope allowed by the zoning. These are the "build it and they will come" capture rates, and they are the maximum possible rates. The other set of capture rates reflects the share of population and employment growth needed just to cover the cost of infrastructure. In finance terms, these capture rates generate a return on investment of 1.0 and an NPV of 0. Usually, capture rates from the return on investment analysis would be less than the maximum rates but more than the breakeven rates. The suggested approach to estimating population and employment capture rates follows.

Maximum Capture Rates

Development Equivalents

- Assume that the development envelope will be completely built and occupied over the time horizon.
- Translate the build-out scenario into the number of dwelling units and amount of commercial space.

Population and Employment Estimates

- Equate the number of dwelling units to households.
- Estimate population for the relevant time period by multiplying the number of households by the best estimate of household size (persons per household).
- Estimate employment for the relevant time period by dividing the amount of commercial space by the best estimate of space in square feet per employee.

Capture Rates

- Divide the population estimate by the forecast of population growth for the urban or metro area over the relevant time period.
- Divide the employment estimate by the forecast of employment growth for the urban or metro area over this time period.

Breakeven Capture Rates

Development Equivalents

- Treat the cost of infrastructure as the minimum acceptable value of future tax revenues.

- Divide this amount by the current tax rate to find the total assessed value, which is equivalent to the cost of new development.
- Allocate assessed value to housing or commercial development by using the mix and intensity reflected in the proposed zoning for the small area.
- Translate these values into the equivalent number of dwelling units and amount of commercial space.

Population and Employment Estimates
- Equate the number of dwelling units to households.
- Estimate population for the relevant time period by multiplying the number of households by the best estimate of household size (persons per household).
- Estimate employment for the relevant time period by dividing the amount of commercial space by the best estimate of space in square feet per employee.

Capture Rates
- Divide the population estimate by the forecast of population growth for the urban or metro area over the relevant time period.
- Divide the employment estimate by the forecast of employment growth for the urban or metro area over this time period.

Commentary on Risk Assessment

Capture rates are frequently used in real estate market analysis to gauge risk: the lower the capture rates, the lower the risk. These population and employment capture rates provide two different insights. The maximum capture rates indicate how much growth, in terms of percentage share, is required to fill the development envelope. The breakeven capture rates indicate the minimum share of growth needed to cover the cost of public infrastructure.

Capture rates computed in this manner can be used to compare infrastructure investments for several areas at one point in time or for one area for different time periods.

Notes

Chapter 1: Introduction: Challenges to Sustainable Urban Growth

1. See Urban Land Institute, http://urbanland.uli.org/Sustainability; American Planning Association, www.planning.org/policy/guides/adopted/sustainability.htm; American Institute of Architects, www.aia.org/about/initiatives/AIAS075425; and ICLEI—Local Governments for Sustainability, www.icleiusa.org/library/documents/STAR_Sustainability_Goals.pdf.

2. Developers' pro formas are spreadsheets that keep track of financial information to determine financial feasibility. Financial returns are the amount or rate of cash funds derived from a completed development project. If return on invested equity appears attractive, the developer is likely to pursue the project.

Chapter 2: Design, Development, and Regulation Silos

1. Return on investment is measured in static terms and dynamic terms. The cash-on-cash return is the amount received after all obligations are met per dollar of invested equity. This static return is measured when the project achieves stabilized occupancy, usually 90–95 percent. The dynamic return measures, net present value and internal rate of return, are defined in chapter 6. Investors who purchase an existing property receive cash flow because they own an operating enterprise with tenants. Developers can only estimate returns because they have a development idea yet to be realized, from which cash flow may be derived at some future time.

2. See www.icleiusa.org/sustainability/star-community-index. See also Brueggeman and Fisher 2011.

3. See www.usgbc.org.

4. See www.formbasedcodes.org.

5. Multiplier models estimate the results of consecutive rounds of buying and selling that arise from an initial project stimulus.

Chapter 4: Apartment Project Alternatives

1. See www.rsmeans.com.

Chapter 6: Dynamic Financial Analysis

1. Discounted cash flow analysis is conducted on a cash basis of accounting, as is revenue-expense analysis, instead of on an accrual basis.

Chapter 7: Infill Redevelopment Alternatives

1. This case is based on the proposed redevelopment of the Glen Lennox rental housing and community commercial project. Its materials are used with the permission of its owner, Grubb Properties, and their consultant firms. The development regulations are those of the Town of Chapel Hill Planning Department.

2. Development of income-generating property becomes similar to development of for-sale residential when the developer decides to "flip" an income-generating project. In that case, the developer sells the project as soon as stabilized occupancy is achieved. The hold period is eliminated, and the permanent loan becomes unnecessary; the proceeds from the sale are used to repay the construction loan.

3. The construction loan amount shown in the capital budget is $125.25 million. When the permanent loans for the retail and office development begin, these loans "take out" the equivalent amount of construction loan. The actual remaining construction loan balance with these deductions is $46.072 million. The slight discrepancy is due to simplifying assumptions made about the timing of development.

4. Retail rents are often charged on a triple net basis, meaning that the tenant pays for property insurance, real estate taxes, and most operating expenses. Office rents are often charged on a gross basis, meaning that the owner pays for virtually all operating expenses.

5. See www.costar.com.

6. See www.irr.com/Publication/PublicationList.asp.

7. See Form-Based Codes Institute, www.formbasedcodes.org.

Chapter 8: Development Coordination Recommendations

1. See www.ncppp.org.

Glossary of Real Estate Development Terms

This glossary defines terms used in the discussion of the developer's financial calculations throughout this book and illustrated in the examples in the appendices to chapters 3 and 6. All terms in the glossary are listed alphabetically in the index.

acquisition: The purchase of a vacant site or a site with buildings on it.

building area: The building area is measured in two ways. *Gross building area* (GBA) is the actual size of the building measured by its exterior perimeter. *Gross rentable area* (GRA), which is also called *net leasable area* (NLA), is the internal space occupied by tenants for their exclusive use.

capital budget: The capital budget is the financial statement that shows the total cost of a development project. The major cost categories are the land or site acquisition cost, site development costs, hard costs, and soft costs.

- *hard costs*: Construction costs, including foundations, shell and roofing, interior finishes, systems (HVAC, plumbing, electrical), installed equipment, and all associated labor.
- *site development costs*: Costs associated with land disturbance (grubbing, trenching, grading, cutting and filling); open space; infrastructure (water system, sanitary and storm sewers, gas, fiber optic cable, telephone, electricity, other subsurface utilities); circulation (streets, sidewalks, specific bike or pedestrian access, and rights-of-way); lighting; signage; parking areas; and landscaping (trees, shrubs, other vegetation, grass, sod, xeriscape alternatives).
- *soft costs*: Fees for the contractor; costs of architecture and engineering, landscape architecture and land planning, appraisals, market analysis and marketing, legal and accounting services; costs associated with development project review (application fees and permits, inspection fees, tap fees, impact fees, cost of impact studies); costs of site assessment (environmental studies, title search, property survey, tax recording); debt-related financing costs, including closing costs and construction-period interest, and costs of documentation and filings required to raise equity and establish legal ownership; and costs of other items, including insurance, bonds, property taxes during construction, developer profit, and contingency.

capitalization rate: The market-determined capitalization rate is the average return measured as net operating income (NOI) from one dollar invested in a specific investment property type. There are capitalization rates for apartments, hotels, industrial buildings, offices, retail buildings, and other investment properties. When a property is purchased or developed, the *going-in* capitalization rate is the NOI at stabilized occupancy divided by the investment or cost of development. The *going-out* capitalization rate is the rate used to estimate the value of the property to be sold. It is higher than the going-in rate to reflect both the uncertain future and the obsolescence that occurs to buildings with the passage of time.

cash flows: There are two primary types of cash flows: those from operations and those from disposition. Cash flows from operations, also called property cash flows, are the cash returns that occur while the owner or developer holds the property. Cash flows from disposition occur after the owner successfully sells the property. A third type, tax cash flows, accounts for income tax liability under IRS regulations.

cash flows from disposition: These include property cash flows and tax cash flows. These cash flows account for the sale of the property.

- *gross sales price (GSP)*: The amount received for the sale of the property. The best estimate of the expected GSP is derived by dividing the estimated net operating income (NOI) for the year after the hold period ends by the terminal, or going-out, capitalization rate to estimate value.
- *selling expenses (SE)*: A percentage of the gross sales price, usually 6 percent or less on larger transactions.
- *net sales price (NSP)*: Found by subtracting selling expenses from the gross sales price.
- *unpaid mortgage balance (UM)*: The balance remaining at the end of the hold period. Under financing cash flows, the mortgage balance is taken from the amortization table.
- *before-tax equity reversion (BTER)*: The difference between the net sales price and unpaid mortgage balance. It is the amount of equity due to the owner. It is also called the residual.
- *original development cost or investment (OC)*: The amount of money spent to develop or purchase the property, the OC is needed to calculate the tax on capital gain. Major investments made during the hold period are added to the OC and reduce the gain.
- *capital gain (GAIN)*: The difference between the net sales price and

original development cost. It reflects property appreciation over the hold period.

- *capital gains rate (CGR)*: The tax rate on long-term gains. It is currently 15 percent.
- *capital gains tax (CGTAX)*: Calculated by multiplying the 15 percent capital gains rate by the capital gain. The other tax owed is the *recapture tax*.
- *accumulated depreciation (ACCDEP)*: The sum of the annual amount of depreciation taken during the hold period.
- *recapture tax rate (RCR)*: Currently 25 percent.
- *recapture tax (RECTAX)*: The recapture tax rate multiplied by accumulated depreciation.
- *total tax (TOTTAX)*: The amount of taxes due to the IRS from the sale of a property. This is calculated by adding the capital gains tax and recapture tax.
- *after-tax equity reversion (ATER)*: The amount the investor has left from the sale after paying the total tax.

construction: The process of building on a vacant site or renovating an improved site.

debt capital: The following terms describe how debt capital is dealt with in investment analysis.

- *loan-to-cost ratio*: The amount of the loan (debt capital) as a fraction of the total cost of the project shown in the capital budget. It is similar to the loan-to-value ratio, which is the fraction of the loan to the value of the project. The loan-to-cost ratio is used to underwrite development projects; the loan-to-value ratio is used to evaluate real estate investments in established projects.
- *debt service (DS)*: The amount of the loan, the frequency of payments (usually monthly), the length or term of the loan, and the interest rate charged generate the monthly debt service required to amortize the loan. The loan is amortized by paying interest each period plus some amount of principal. Although

the debt-service payment remains constant over the term of the loan, the amount of interest decreases, and principal repayment increases over time.

- *debt-service coverage ratio (DSCR)*: Net operating income (NOI) divided by debt service. Net operating income is expected to exceed debt service to provide a cushion for revenue shortfalls. A typical DSCR is 1.2, indicating that NOI is 20 percent greater than debt service. For example, if a project's net revenues are $120,000, and its debt-service payment is $100,000, then its DSCR is 1.2. The lender establishes the target DSCR to reflect the risks of the project as well as general market conditions. The DSCR increases with project risk.
- *mortgage constant*: The cost of one dollar of debt per payment period, which depends on the interest rate charged, the loan term (number of months or years), and the frequency of repayment. If the loan was interest-only and paid once each year, the annual mortgage constant would be the same as the interest rate charged for the loan. Most loans are amortizing—which means that some principal is paid back, as well as interest—and are paid monthly. The monthly mortgage constant is the fraction of the loan paid off each month, which includes both principal and interest. The constant debt-service amount paid each period is found by multiplying the mortgage constant by the original loan amount. Note that since cost-driven and market-driven analyses are annual analyses, it is necessary to multiply the monthly mortgage constant by 12 to get the annualized monthly mortgage constant.

development envelope analysis: Application of zoning and other regulations and physical constraints of the site to determine the maximum intensity of use in terms of units and square footage (both floor area and volume).

efficiency ratio: This is the ratio of gross rentable area divided by gross building area.

equity capital: The following terms define how equity capital is treated in investment analysis.

- *before tax cash-on-cash returns*: The return on investment expected by those investing in the project. This return represents the cost of equity to the developer. A cash-on-cash return of 12 percent indicates that investors expect to receive $12 for each $100 invested in the project.
- *before-tax cash flow (BTCF)*: The cash flow remaining after debt service is subtracted from net operating income.

financial plan: The capital budget indicates the intended uses of funds; the financial plan shows the intended sources of funds. *Equity capital* is the source of funds provided by the owners of the project; *debt capital* is the amount of other people's money available in the form of loans to the project owners. See separate entries for these two terms for definitions of other financing terms related to each form of capital.

market analysis: An assessment of the existing rents and vacancies in the local market. Formal market analysis forecasts the future relationships between supply and demand in local market areas. If forecast demand exceeds anticipated supply, the excess may be large enough to support the planned amount of new supply in the development project. Real estate market analysis is more art than science because demand is hard to forecast, long-term supply is even more difficult to forecast, and real estate and business cycles affect rent levels and trends.

property cash flows: The returns from the development project operations. Their calculation includes:

- *gross potential revenue (GPR)*: Total leasable units or space multiplied by the unit rent. The amount of space available to lease is called *net leasable area*, or gross rentable area. The *efficiency ratio* is multiplied by gross building area to find the amount that can be rented to tenants. Some projects have additional sources of revenue (for example, from renting common facilities or charging for vending or other services) that are added to revenue from space rental.

- *vacancy allowance (VAC)*: The amount of revenue lost due to vacant space or nonpayment of rent. Because frictional vacancy (due to different timing of move-ins and move-outs) is expected even in the highest-performing project, some vacancy allowance is always included.
- *effective gross income (EGI)*: The difference between gross potential revenue and vacancy allowance.
- *operating expenses (OEX)*: The expenses incurred to manage and operate the property, such as property insurance and utility charges, routine repairs and maintenance, and payment of real property taxes. Real estate taxes are often treated separately because they are determined by the local jurisdiction and not the managers of the project.
- *net operating income (NOI)*: The difference between effective gross income and operating expenses. Net operating income is the amount of revenue the owner expects to clear from operating the property.

tax cash flows: These calculations are necessary because income from property ownership is subject to taxation.

- *IRS Books*: The accounts that the owner uses to keep track of income tax liability.
- *interest (INT)*: The interest portion of debt service paid.
- *depreciation (DEP)*: A nonmonetary expense allowed to be deducted from income in recognition that the property is being "used up" and becoming obsolete over time. Currently, the IRS allows owners of residential property to depreciate or write off value proportionately for 27.5 years. Owners of commercial property have to depreciate their property more slowly, over 39 years.
- *taxable income (TI)*: Calculated by subtracting interest and depreciation from net operating income.

- *Investor's Books*: Accounts used by an investor to calculate his or her financial position after income taxes are paid.
- *marginal tax rate (MTR)*: The owner's marginal income tax rate, which is assumed to be 33 percent.
- *tax liability (TAX)*: The calculated amount of taxes due to the IRS, found by multiplying taxable income by the owner's marginal tax rate.
- *after-tax cash flow (ATCF)*: The amount left after the tax liability is paid from *before-tax cash flow*, as defined above.

References

Anderson, Larz. 1995. *Guidelines for Preparing Urban Plans.* Chicago: APA Planners Press.

Appraisal Institute. 2011. *The Appraisal of Real Estate. 14th ed.* Chicago: Appraisal Institute.

Bartholomew, Keith, and Reid Ewing. 2009. "Land Use—Transportation Scenarios and Future Vehicle Travel and Land Consumption: A Meta-Analysis." *Journal of the American Planning Association* 75 (1): 1–15.

Berke, Philip R., David R. Godschalk, and Edward J. Kaiser, with Daniel A. Rodriguez. 2006. *Urban Land Use Planning.* Urbana, Ill.: University of Illinois Press.

Bohl, Charles C. 2002. *Place Making: Developing Town Centers, Main Streets, and Urban Villages.* Washington, D.C.: Urban Land Institute.

Brueggeman, William B., and Jeffrey D. Fisher. 2011. *Real Estate Finance and Investments.* 14th ed. New York: McGraw-Hill Irwin.

Burton, Elizabeth, Mike Jenks, and Katie Williams, eds. 2000. *Achieving Sustainable Urban Form.* London: Routledge.

Carrboro, North Carolina, Town of. 2009. Land Use Ordinance. Article XIII: Recreational Facilities and Open Space. www.ci.carrboro.nc.us/pzi/PDFs/LUO/Art-xiii.pdf.

Carn, Neil, Joseph Rabianski, Ronald Racster, and Maury Seldin. 1988. *Real Estate Market Analysis.* Englewood Cliffs, N.J.: Prentice Hall.

Chakrabarti, Vishaan. 2013. *A Country of Cities: A Manifesto for Urban America.* New York: Metropolis Books.

Ciochetti, Brian A., and Emil E. Malizia. 2000. "The Application of Financial Analysis and Market Research to the Real Estate Development Process." In *Essays in Honor of James A. Graaskamp: Ten Years After*, edited by James DeLisle and Elaine Worzala, 135–65. Boston: Kluwer Academic Publishers.

Condon, Patrick, Duncan Cavens, and Nicole Miller. 2009. *Urban Planning Tools for Climate Change Mitigation.* Boston: Lincoln Institute of Land Policy.

Dinep, Claudia, and Kristin Schwab. 2010. *Sustainable Site Design: Criteria, Process, and Case Studies for Integrating Site and Region in Landscape Design.* Hoboken, N.J.: John Wiley & Sons, Inc.

Dunham-Jones, Ellen, and June Williamson. 2011. *Retrofitting Suburbia: Urban Design Solutions for Redesigning Suburbs.* Updated ed. Hoboken, N.J.: John Wiley & Sons, Inc.

Elliott, Donald L., Matthew Goebel, and Chad Meadows. 2012. *The Rules That Shape Urban Form.* PAS Report 570. Chicago: American Planning Association.

Fanning, Stephen F. 2005. *Market Analysis for Real Estate.* Chicago: Appraisal Institute.

Feiden, Wayne M., with Elisabeth Hamin. 2011. *Assessing Sustainability: A Guide for Local Governments.* PAS Report 565. Chicago: American Planning Association.

Forsyth, Ann. 2005. *Reforming Suburbia: The Planned Communities of Irvine, Columbia, and The Woodlands.* Berkeley: University of California Press.

Godschalk, David R., and William R. Anderson. 2012. *Sustaining Places: The Role of the Comprehensive Plan.* PAS Report 567. Chicago: American Planning Association.

Graaskamp, James A. 1970. *A Guide to Feasibility Analysis*. Chicago: Society of Real Estate Appraisers.

———. 1981. *Fundamentals of Real Estate Development*. Washington, D.C.: Urban Land Institute.

Hall, K., and G. Porterfield. 2001. *Community by Design: New Urbanism for Suburbs and Small Communities*. New York: McGraw-Hill.

Hosack, Walter. 2010. *Land Development Calculation: Interactive Tools for Site Planning, Analysis, and Design*. 2nd ed. New York: McGraw-Hill.

Kelly, Eric Damian. 2009. *Community Planning: An Introduction to the Comprehensive Plan*. 2nd ed. Washington, D.C.: Island Press.

LaGro, James A., Jr. 2008. *Site Analysis: A Contextual Approach to Sustainable Land Planning and Site Design*. 2nd ed. Hoboken, N.J.: John Wiley & Sons, Inc.

Lamont, W. 1979. "Subdivision Regulation and Land Conversion." In *The Practice of Local Government Planning*, edited by F. S. So, I. Stollman, F. Beal, and D. S. Arnold, 389–415. Washington, D.C.: International City Management Association.

Lu, Weiming. 2013. *The Tao of Urban Rejuvenation: Lessons in Building a Creative Urban Village*. Edina, Minn.: Beaver's Pond Press.

Lynch, Kevin, and Gary Hack. 1984. *Site Planning*. 3rd ed. Cambridge, Mass.: MIT Press.

Miles, Mike E., Emil E. Malizia, Marc A. Weiss, Gayle Behrens, and Ginger Travis. 1991. *Real Estate Development: Principles and Process*. Washington, D.C.: Urban Land Institute.

Peca, Stephen. 2009. *Real Estate Development and Investment: A Comprehensive Approach*. Hoboken, N.J.: John Wiley & Sons, Inc.

Peiser, Richard B., and David Hamilton. 2012. *Professional Real Estate Development: The ULI Guide to the Business*. 3rd ed. Washington, D.C.: Urban Land Institute.

Reston Town Center Association. "Reston Town Center History." Accessed March 18, 2013. www.restontc.org/history.html.

Russ, Thomas. 2009. *Site Planning and Design Handbook*. 2nd ed. New York: McGraw-Hill.

Sarté, S. Bry. 2010. *Sustainable Infrastructure: The Guide to Green Engineering and Design*. Hoboken, N.J.: John Wiley & Sons, Inc.

Simonds, John O., and Barry Starke. 2006. *Landscape Architecture: A Manual of Site Planning and Design*. 4th ed. New York: McGraw-Hill.

Solnit, Albert. 1983. P*roject Approval: A Developer's Guide to Successful Local Government Review*. Belmont, Calif.: Wadsworth Publishing Company/Continuing Education.

Talen, Emily. 2012. *City Rules: How Regulations Affect Urban Form*. Washington, D.C.: Island Press.

Urban Design Associates. 2012. Glen Lennox Area Neighborhood Conservation District Plan for CD-8C. Accessed September 18, 2013. http://www.townofchapelhill.org/Modules/ShowDocument.aspx?documentid=13994.

U.S. Green Building Council. 2012. "LEED for Neighborhood Development." Accessed May 21, 2013. www.usgbc.org/neighborhoods.

Williamson, June. 2013. *Designing Suburban Futures: New Models from Build a Better Burb*. Washington, D.C.: Island Press.

Index

About the Authors

David R. Godschalk, FAICP, is Stephen Baxter Professor Emeritus in the Department of City and Regional Planning at the University of North Carolina at Chapel Hill. A Fellow of the American Institute of Certified Planners, he has been a professional planner and a planning educator, publishing 12 books on the topics of:

- growth management, land-use planning, and sustainable development;
- natural hazard mitigation and coastal management; and
- development dispute resolution, public participation, and collaborative planning.

His recent publications are: *The Dynamic Decade: Creating the Sustainable Campus for the University of North Carolina at Chapel Hill, 2001–2011* (University of North Carolina Press, 2012) and *Sustaining Places: The Role of the Comprehensive Plan* (APA Planners Press, 2012). His coauthored text *Urban Land Use Planning* (University of Illinois Press, 2006) is in its fifth edition. Godschalk chaired the 2013 APA Working Group on Comprehensive Plan Certification, cochaired the 2011 APA Sustaining Places Task Force, and served on the Chapel Hill Town Council and the North Carolina Smart Growth Commission. He was editor of the *Journal of the American Institute of Planners*, vice president of a Tampa planning consulting firm, and planning director of Gainesville, Florida. He holds degrees from Dartmouth College, the University of Florida, and the University of North Carolina. He is a registered architect (inactive) in Florida.

Emil E. Malizia, FAICP, is Professor in the Department of City and Regional Planning at the University of North Carolina at Chapel Hill. His expertise spans the related areas of regional economic development, real estate development, and urban redevelopment. For more than four decades, he has conducted research, taught graduate-level and in-service courses, and engaged in consulting for private, nonprofit, and public clients.

He is the author or coauthor of five books and more than 150 scholarly articles, monographs, and other publications. He has been a senior real estate adviser to a major life insurance company, a visiting professor, a special assistant in federal service, and a Fulbright Scholar (Colombia). He is a member of the American Planning Association, American Real Estate Society, International Economic Development Council, and Urban Land Institute. He received his baccalaureate from Rutgers University and his master's and doctoral degrees from Cornell University.